RACE MEN

HAZEL V. CARBY

HARVARD UNIVERSITY PRESS

*Cambridge, Massachusetts
and London, England*
1998

Excerpts from "American Hero," "Heavy Breathing," "I Want to Talk about You,"
"When My Brother Fell," are from *Ceremonies*, by Essex Hemphill.
Copyright © 1992 by Essex Hemphill. Used by permission of Dutton Signet,
a division of Penguin Books USA Inc.

Library of Congress Cataloging-in-Publication Data
Carby, Hazel V.
Race men / Hazel V. Carby.
p. cm. — (The W.E.B. Du Bois lectures)
Includes index.
ISBN 0-674-74558-2 (alk. paper)
1. Afro-American men in popular culture.
2. Masculinity in popular culture—United States.
I. Title. II.Series.
E185.86.C297   1998
305.38′896073—dc21
98-14077

RACE MEN

The W. E. B. Du Bois Lectures

*For my son, Nicholas, who will, I hope, live
in more liberated and egalitarian times*

CONTENTS

RACE MEN

INTRODUCTION

[S]ince the dominant view holds prideful self-respect as the very essence of healthy African American identity, it also considers such identity to be fundamentally weakened wherever masculinity appears to be
compromised. While this fact is rarely articulated, its influence is
nonetheless real and pervasive. Its primary effect is that all debates
over and claims to "authentic" African-American identity are largely
animated by a profound anxiety about the status specifically of African-American *masculinity*.

Phillip Brian Harper

In these days of what is referred to as "global culture," the Nike
corporation produces racialized images for the world by elevating the
bodies of Michael Jordan and Tiger Woods to the status of international icons. Hollywood too now takes for granted that black bodies can
be used to promote both products and style worldwide, and an increasing number of their "black" films are being produced and directed by
black men. But despite the multimillion-dollar international trade in
black male bodies, and encouragement to "just do it," there is no
equivalent in international outrage, no marches or large-scale public
protest, at the hundreds of thousands of black male bodies languishing
out of sight of the media in the North American penal system.

Between the time that W. E. B. Du Bois published *The Souls of Black
Folk*, discussed in the first chapter, and Danny Glover gained the status
of international superstar in the *Lethal Weapon* series of films between

1987 and 1992, the subject of the last chapter, there has been a stark reversal in the nature of the visibility of the black male body, if not much of a change in the fortune of most black men. If the spectacle of the lynched black body haunts the modern age, then the slow disintegration of black bodies and souls in jail, urban ghettos, and beleaguered schools haunts our postmodern times.

This book traverses this history and asks questions about the nature of the cultural representation of various black masculinities at different historical moments and in different media: literature, photography, film, music and song. It does not seek to be a comprehensive history of the roles of black men in any one of these cultural forms but considers the cultural and political complexity of particular inscriptions, performances, and enactments of black masculinity on a variety of stages. Each stage is deliberately bounded and limited in its construction.

Ideologies of masculinity always exist in a dialectical relation to other ideologies—I have chosen to focus upon their articulation with discourses of race and nation in American culture. However, rather than analyze these discourses in representations of famous political figures, like Frederick Douglass, Malcolm X, or Martin Luther King, Jr., or through the work of established writers of fiction like Richard Wright, Ralph Ellison, and James Baldwin, I focus on a variety of artists and intellectuals.

For W. E. B. Du Bois, I have constructed the stage upon *The Souls of Black Folk*, because his book has become a canonical text in American culture and because its theory of double-consciousness has been so widely adopted to explain the nature of the African American soul. Though Du Bois led a long and varied intellectual and political life, I have limited his stage to this text because it is so frequently taken to be representative of black intellectual, psychological, and existential reality.

The stage for Paul Robeson, in the second chapter, is limited to the 1920s and 1930s in order to demonstrate the complexities of representations of race and gender within the modernist aesthetic. Robeson came to represent a form of black masculinity against which he eventually rebelled, seeking an alternative political and artistic aesthetic through activism and the Left Theatre Movement in England. (Robeson was perhaps the first internationally acclaimed black icon, and Michael Jordan, Tiger Woods, and Danny Glover would do well to reflect upon the politics of Robeson's response to this fame.) Whereas Du Bois argued for the importance of recognizing the centrality of black people and black culture to the formation of the United States, Robeson rejected the terms and conditions upon which his acclaim depended and, as a result, was declared a threat to national security.

The third chapter considers the stage of the spirituals and American folk song. Du Bois had argued for the historical significance of the sorrow songs, but interpretations of Robeson's performance of the spirituals repressed the history of exploitation and oppression out of which they grew. John and Alan Lomax's search for a representative of the American folk song led them to invent their own version of the dangerous, if gifted, black male, in the person of Huddie Ledbetter, known as Leadbelly, whose voice, though not his person, could be presented to the national archive.

In chapter four I argue that the cricket pitch is the stage upon which we should begin to understand the work of C. L. R. James. His cricket journalism recreates the world of body lines and color lines and represents the black male body as both autonomous and inspirational. James's descriptions of cricket as the site where lines of class, race, and gender are forged foreshadows his work on the Haitian revolutionary, Toussaint L'Ouverture.

The misogyny of Miles Davis and the world of jazz in the late 1950s and early 1960s provides the stage for a consideration of an alternative black masculinity performed in his music. Interwoven with this analysis of Davis's life and music is the work of Samuel Delany, a writer who consistently challenges his readers to expand their visions of masculinities and femininities through his revolutionary fiction and criticism.

Lastly, I propose that the film career of Danny Glover traces the development of an important Hollywood narrative of black masculinity. This narrative promises to resolve the racial contradictions and crises of the 1980s and 1990s through a revision of the traditional trope of the black male/white male partnership, a partnership which firmly excludes the democratic participation of women in modern public life.

There remains the question, what is a race man? Clearly, I think that it is a concept that encompasses all of the above, but is also much more than that. For a century, the figure of the race man has haunted black political and cultural thought, and this book seeks to conduct a feminist interrogation of this theme and of other definitions of black masculinity at work in American culture.

In 1945, in *Black Metropolis*, St. Clair Drake and Horace Cayton attempted to account for the emergence of the idea of a race man. "Race consciousness," they asserted, "is not the work of 'agitators,' or 'subversive influences'—it is forced upon Negroes by the very fact of their separate-subordinate status in American life." Since emancipation, Drake and Cayton argue, black people have had to prove, actively and consistently, that they were not the inferior beings that their status as second-class citizens declared them to be: hence an aggressive demonstration of their superiority in some field of achievement, either individually or collectively, was what established race pride: "the success of one Negro" was interpreted as "the success of all." The result of the pursuit of "race consciousness, race pride, and race solidarity" was the emergence of particular social types, among which was the Race Man.[1] Drake and Cayton add this cautionary note, however: "People try to draw a line between 'sincere Race Leaders' and those Race Men who are always clamoring everything for the race, just for the glory of being known."[2] The issue of acting as a race man for particular audiences is still relevant in a society where the mass media all too eagerly assign to a few carefully chosen voices the representation of the racialized many, and the chosen rarely reject their designation and transient moment of glory. What a race man signifies for the white segments of our society is not necessarily how a race man is defined for various black constituencies.[3]

While Drake and Cayton effectively situate the subtleties and complexities produced by and through processes of racialization in the United States, they, along with most contemporary black male intellectuals, take for granted the gendering at work in the other half of the concept "race man"—the part that is limited to man. What we have inherited from them and from others is a rarely questioned notion of masculinity as it is connected to ideas of race and nation.

In 1897, eighteen black men, under the leadership of Alexander Crummell, formally inaugurated the American Negro Academy. In his address to this august assembly, W. E. B. Du Bois declared: "For the development of Negro genius, of Negro literature and art, of Negro spirit, only Negroes bound and welded together, Negroes inspired by one vast ideal, can work out in its fullness the great message we have for humanity."[4] But only black men were to be "bound and welded together." Nothing was done to recruit black women into the Academy.[5]

Nevertheless, Crummell and the Negro Academies continue to stand as emblematic figures for the designation of black intellectual. The historian Wilson J. Moses has recently asserted that the life of Alexander Crummell "symbolizes the intricacy of the experience of black American intellectuals: their conflicting emotions with respect to the Western world, their discontent with 'civilization,' and their dependency on it, as they have labored to impose order on their existence both as racial beings and as individuals."[6] My position in this book is an outright rejection of the male-centered assumptions at work in such claims of representativeness.

In the late 1990s the work of black women intellectuals is still considered peripheral by the black male establishment. It is true that, superficially, the situation appears to have improved. The words "women and gender" are frequently added after the word "race" and the appropriate commas, and increasingly the word "sexuality" completes the litany. On occasion a particular black woman's name will be mentioned, like that of Toni Morrison. But the *intellectual work* of black women and gay men is not thought to be of enough significance to be engaged with, argued with, agreed or disagreed with. Thus terms like women, gender, and sexuality have a decorative function only. They color the background of the canvas to create the appropriate illusion of inclusion and diversity, but they do not affect the shape or texture of the subject.

Indeed, we have recently been told by one of America's leading intellectuals that unless black intellectuals affect the demeanor and attire of the Victorian male in his dark three-piece suit, they will remain marginal and impotent![7]

While contemporary black male intellectuals claim to challenge the hegemony of a racialized social formation, most fail to challenge the hegemony of their own assumptions about black masculinity and accept the consensus of a dominant society that "conceives African American society in terms of a perennial 'crisis' of black masculinity whose imagined solution is a proper affirmation of black male authority."[8] This apparent solution was at work in the Million Man March, but it is also at work in contemporary black intellectual life. On the contrary, rather than continue to dress ourselves in what Essex Hemphill calls "this threadbare masculinity," it is necessary to recognize the complex ways in which black masculinity has been, and still is, socially and culturally produced.

I am eager to burn
this threadbare masculinity
this perpetual black suit
I have outgrown.

ESSEX HEMPHILL

1

THE SOULS OF BLACK MEN

Du Bois is the brook of fire through which we all must pass in order to gain access to the intellectual and political weaponry needed to sustain the radical democratic tradition in our time.

Cornel West

In a grand Victorian gesture of self-sacrifice, W. E. B. Du Bois, then a young man in the formative years of his intellectual development, determined to subordinate his individual desires and ambitions to promote a political project that would benefit the world in general by advancing the particular interests of African American peoples. In his journal entry of February 23, 1893, his twenty-fifth birthday, Du Bois wrote:

> I am striving to make my life all that life may be—and I am limiting that strife only in so far as that strife is incompatible with others of my brothers and sisters making their lives similar. . . . I am firmly convinced that my own best development is not one and the same with the best development of the world and here I am willing to sacrifice. . . . I therefore . . . work for the rise of the Negro people, taking for granted that their best development means the best development of the world.

Du Bois decided, however, that the commitment he undertook did not require him to set aside the interests of selfish desire and ambition: the entry concludes that the advancement of his "race" will be intimately tied to his own personal achievements as an intellectual, a man who wishes to "make a name in science, to make a name in art and thus to raise my race."[1]

Through a close analysis of Du Bois's *The Souls of Black Folk*, I will argue that although he declares that he intends to limit his striving "in so far as that strife is incompatible with others of my brothers and sisters making their lives similar," beneath the surface of this apparent sacrifice of individual desire to become an intellectual and a race leader is a conceptual framework that is gender-specific; not only does it apply exclusively to men, but it encompasses only those men who enact narrowly and rigidly determined codes of masculinity.

This gendered framework negates in fact the opportunity offered in words for black women to make "their lives similar"; the project suffers from Du Bois's complete failure to imagine black women as intellectuals and race leaders. The failure to incorporate black women into the sphere of intellectual equality, I will demonstrate, is not merely the result of the sexism of Du Bois's historical moment, as evident in the language of his chapter titles in *The Souls of Black Folk*, such as "Of the Training of Black Men," and "The Sons of Master and Man."[2] It is a conceptual and political failure of imagination that remains a characteristic of the work of contemporary African American male intellectuals. Du Bois described and challenged the hegemony of the national and racial formations in the United States at the dawn of a new century, but he did so in ways that both assumed and privileged a discourse of black masculinity. Cornel West describes and challenges the hegemony of the national and racial formations at the end of the same century, but many of these discourses are still in place.

In a recent essay, West asserts that Du Bois's "patriarchal sensibilities speak for themselves."[3] On the contrary, I will argue that they do not "speak for themselves" but have to be rigorously examined so that we may follow and grasp their epistemological implications and consequences. West's easy dismissal suggests that there is no need to undertake the serious intellectual work necessary to understand the processes that gender knowledge.

West sets up three fundamental pillars of Du Bois's intellectual project: his "Enlightenment world view"; his "Victorian strategies" (the way his world view is translated into practice); and his "American optimism."[4] Is there no need to understand how these foundations articulate with ideologies of gender? If "patriarchal sensibilities speak for themselves," then they are merely superficial, easily recognized, and quickly accounted for, enabling real intellectual work to continue elsewhere.[5] If they "speak for themselves," then nothing of intellectual value or worth could result from demonstrating or exposing exactly what constitutes "patriarchy" or "patriarchal sensibilities." It is through such devices that members of the contemporary black male intellectual establishment, sometimes referred to by the media as "the new black intellectuals," disregard the need for feminist analysis while maintaining a politically correct posture of making an obligatory, though finally empty, gesture toward it.[6]

Du Bois constructed particular personal, political, and social characteristics of a racialized masculinity to articulate his definition of black leadership. He was particularly concerned about the "moral uplift of a people" and felt that this was best accomplished "by planting in every community of Negroes black men with ideals of life and thrift and civilization, such as must in time filter through the masses and set examples of moral living."[7] After weighing the political and social needs of what he imagined to be the race, he judged the worth of black male intellectuals and would-be race leaders according to those needs. In addition to focusing on that discussion, my analysis of *The Souls of Black Folk* will demonstrate how, in a similar fashion, Du Bois measured, judged, and lived his own multifaceted identity—as a black intellectual, as a race leader, and as a man. It is important not only to recognize the varied and complex ways in which Du Bois developed a public persona that was crafted to embody the philosophy he espoused, but also to analyze the ideological effect of such embodiment on his philosophic judgments. My contention is that these judgments reveal highly gendered structures of intellectual and political thought and feeling; these structures are embedded in specific ways in *The Souls of Black Folk*, first published in 1903, reprinted twenty-four times by 1940, revived in the 1960s and 1970s, and now regarded as a founding text in the study of black culture.[8]

First, let me anticipate and address possible objections to the feminist politics of this project. I decided to analyze the intellectual and political thought and feeling of *The Souls of Black Folk* from the perspective of its gendered structure precisely because it *is* such an important intellectual work. I absolutely agree with Wesley Brown that "Politically, Du Bois's activism always seem to anticipate struggles that followed . . . his crucial role in the formation of the N.A.A.C.P., the Pan African Movement, and the efforts to ban nuclear weapons paved the way for our own participation in the Civil Rights Movement and the Vietnam war protests of the nineteen sixties. This link between Du Bois and struggles for self determination continues until this day."[9]

I do not focus on *The Souls of Black Folk* because I feel that it is a particularly egregious example of sexist thinking; it isn't. Nor is it my intention to claim that W. E. B. Du Bois was a sexist male individual. In the public arena, as an African American intellectual and as a politician, Du Bois advocated equality for women and consistently supported feminist causes later in his life.

There is, unfortunately, no simple correspondence between anyone's support for female equality and the ideological effect of the gendered structures of thought and feeling at work in any text one might write and publish.[10] If, as intellectuals and as activists, we are committed, like Du Bois, to struggles for liberation and democratic egalitarianism, then surely it is not contradictory also to struggle to be critically aware of the ways in which ideologies of gender have undermined our egalitarian visions in the past and continue to do so in the present. Gendered structures of thought and feeling permeate our lives and our intellectual work, including *The Souls of Black Folk* and other texts which have been regarded as *founding* texts written by the *founding fathers* of black American history and culture.

In the North American and European academies, Du Bois has come to embody the ideal or representative figure of the African American intellectual, "the brook of fire through which we all must pass in order to gain access to the intellectual and political weaponry needed to sustain the radical democratic tradition in our time."[11] If we agree that our critical practice ought to include probing the various ways in which we constitute our fields of knowledge, I contend that we need to expose and learn from the gendered, ideological assumptions which underlie the founding texts and determine that their authors become the *representative* figures of the American intellectual. These authors and their productions are shaped by gendered structures of thought and feeling, which in turn actively shape the major paradigms and modes of thought of all academic discourse.

The significance of *The Souls of Black Folk* as a text which offered new and alternative ways to formulate complex issues of race and nation was immediately recognized by black intellectuals when it was first published in 1903.[12] In *The Autobiography of an Ex-Colored Man* (1912), James Weldon Johnson paid homage to *The Souls of Black Folk* as offering the country something previously unknown "in depicting the life, the ambitions, the struggles, and the passions of those of their race who are striving to break the narrow limits of traditions."[13] In his autobiography *Along This Way*, first published in 1933, Johnson asserted that *The Souls of Black Folk* "had a greater effect upon and within the Negro race in America than any other single book published in this country since *Uncle Tom's Cabin*."[14]

Johnson's enthusiasm was kindled by the ambitious attempt of *The Souls of Black Folk* to create a genealogy for what Benedict Anderson has called an "*imagined community* among a specific assemblage of fellow readers."[15] Through its representations of individuals, Du Bois's book aims to bring into being a community. Imaginatively, he forges a people from his articulation of the material terms of their historical existence.[16]

Because *The Souls of Black Folk* was so successful in the creation and imagining of a black community, it was an important text to academics and political activists outside of the academy who fought to establish African American Studies as a coherent and structured field of knowledge—a process which also needed to bring its own imagined community into being through the intellectual and political work of identifying intellectual ancestors; situating and classifying their texts; establishing literary canons and genres of writing; and establishing traditions of thought and intellectual practice.

As one of these rediscovered ancestors, Du Bois became many things to many people: in response to the needs of various agendas, he was situated as an important precursor of different traditions and strands of thought. For Houston Baker, for example, *The Souls of Black Folk* established the general significance of Du Bois as "the black man of culture"; Darwin Turner has argued for the importance of situating Du Bois in relation to a theory of a "Black Aesthetic"; and Wilson J. Moses has stressed the importance of Du Bois's poetics of "Ethiopianism" in order to position him as an important figure in a tradition of "literary black nationalism."[17] As a literary critic, Arnold Rampersad believes that

> The greatness of *The Souls of Black Folk* as a document of black American culture lies in its creation of profound and enduring myths about the life of the people. . . . If all of a nation's literature may stem from one book, as Hemingway implied about *The Adventures of Huckleberry Finn*, then it can as accurately be said that all of Afro-American literature of a creative nature has proceeded from Du Bois' comprehensive statement on the nature of the people in *The Souls of Black Folk*.[18]

Similarly, Robert Stepto has defined the African American literary canon as those texts which expressed a "primary pregeneric myth of . . . the quest for freedom and literacy," and positioned *The Souls of Black Folk* as "a seminal text in Afro-American letters."[19] "Seminal" is, perhaps, the most appropriate (if gendered) adjective to describe the present canonic status of *The Souls of Black Folk*, not just as a work of literature but also as a major contribution to the study of African American history, sociology, politics, and philosophy.[20]

Perhaps the most influential contemporary recovery of Du Bois as a major influence in African American intellectual thought and practice is the work of Cornel West.[21] In West's opinion "W. E. B. Du Bois is the towering black scholar of the twentieth century. The scope of his interests, the depth of his insights, and the sheer majesty of his prolific writings bespeak a level of genius unequaled among modern black intellectuals."[22] In addition to being considered the *greatest* American intellectual of African descent, Du Bois is also the *only* African American intellectual whom West includes in his *The American Evasion of Philosophy: A Genealogy of Pragmatism.*[23]

In this book West argues that pragmatism is a viable and necessary alternative to epistemology-centered philosophy. Pragmatism, he proposes, is "a conception of philosophy as a form of cultural criticism in which the meaning of America is put forward by intellectuals in response to distinct social and cultural crises." As a form of cultural criticism, "American pragmatism is less a philosophical tradition putting forward solutions to perennial problems in the Western philosophical conversation initiated by Plato and more a continuous cultural commentary or set of interpretations that attempt to explain America to itself at a particular historical moment." West situates his own intellectual work within this tradition and sees himself as a direct descendant of the form of cultural criticism which he has thus defined.[24] And, because Du Bois is the only other black intellectual in this schema, he is West's only representative African American ancestor.

For West, the ideal black intellectual acts as a "critical organic catalyst," a practitioner of "prophetic criticism,"[25] and someone who can become, as West regards himself, "a race-transcending prophet."[26] While all of West's books both criticize and praise the work and ideas of a wide range of intellectuals, only Du Bois is consistently present in all of his texts and the focus of most of the analysis. West self-consciously situates himself as a contemporary embodiment of Du Bois, but he neglects to interrogate the ideological and political *effects* of the gendered nature of Du Bois's theoretical paradigms.

It is a necessary critical task, then, to examine the gendered intellectual practices which structure the way *The Souls of Black Folk* imagines a community and organizes its "framework of consciousness," its "soul."[27] Du Bois creates this community through a complex evocation of the concepts of race, nation, and masculinity.[28] My discussion of the gendering of Du Bois's genealogy of race, of nation, and of manhood will evolve from an analysis of the general narrative structure of the essays and a consideration of the order in which they occur.

If African American writing in North America has its source in the eighteenth- and nineteenth-century texts now identified collectively and variously as slave narratives, personal histories, and spiritual or secular autobiographical texts that give voice to and authenticate black existence, then the narrative structure and genealogy of race, nation, and manhood to be found in *The Souls of Black Folk* imagines its community by reversing the direction of the archetypal journey of these original narratives. The conventional movement of the earlier narratives is away from the conditions of physical and/or mental bondage or despair associated historically with the political, economic, and social formation of the southern states, and toward the attainment of physical and spiritual freedom in the North.[29] But what is understood to be a literary convention has specific political effects: as these narratives moved away from the context in which the majority of African American peoples lived and moved toward a predominantly white society, the direction of the journey determined the imaginative and symbolic landscape in which the conscious desires and ambitions of black humanity could be created and asserted.

Before 1865 it was difficult, if not impossible, for black writers even to imagine the option of returning to the South once black humanity and freedom had been gained in the North. Even after emancipation the American literary imagination was shackled in this respect. For as Mark Twain acknowledged in his 1885 *Adventures of Huckleberry Finn*, once Huck and Jim missed the Ohio river and sailed deeper and deeper into the South, it was necessary for Jim to "belong" to someone, he could no longer belong to himself and survive. As Huck replied when asked if Jim was an escaped slave, "Goodness sakes, would a runaway nigger run *south?*"[30]

In 1903, W. E. B. Du Bois confronted the political dilemmas of previous American narrative forms while also revising many of the conventional concerns expressed in African American literature. The trajectory of *The Souls of Black Folk* is toward the Black Belt of the South, but the text does enact two cultural imperatives from earlier African American literature: freedom and knowledge.[31] The desire for freedom in *The Souls of Black Folk* is a dual quest, both spiritual and physical, while the desire for knowledge emerges in a number of different ways: it is at various times practical, political, philosophical, and spiritual. The text consistently shifts between a predominantly white and a predominantly black world, but its overall narrative impulse gradually moves the focus from a white terrain to an autonomous black one.

Out of a total of fourteen chapters that comprise *The Souls of Black Folk*, nine had been previously published as essays in journals, four of them in *The Atlantic Monthly*. When Du Bois organized them into a book, he did not put them in chronological order according to previous dates of publication or in the order in which he had written them, but arranged them according to an interesting set of themes.[32] Two thirds of the book, the first nine chapters, imagine a black community in relation to its negotiations with the white world of the text. Chapter one, "Of Our Spiritual Strivings," provocatively poses the question that white America dare not ask of black Americans: "How does it feel to be a problem?" It then sets up the existential lament, "Why did God make me an outcast and a stranger in mine own house?" to which the following eight chapters provide the response. Readers are guided through the history and stark present realities of relations of dominance and subordination at the "dawn" of the twentieth century. The story that Du Bois outlines is a story of disappointment, "a vain search for freedom" (p. 48).

The history of this disappointment structures the progress of

Du Bois's genealogy, a narrative which is organized through various struggles to claim national citizenship for black people: struggles to emancipate the slaves; struggles to gain the right to vote; struggles for access to education; and the ever-present struggle against economic inequality. Du Bois reconstructs this history in order to envision an alternative future for the nation.[33] In addition to responding to the questions raised in the first chapter, each of the following eight chapters sets up a call: are all these struggles meaningless for black men? The final third of the book, the last five chapters, answer the call with a clear and resounding "no."

The structure of *The Souls of Black Folk* might be described as what Benedict Anderson calls "an idea of steady, solid simultaneity through time."[34] The political meanings to be derived from this form of organization are embodied in number of individual figures. Du Bois uses anonymous metaphorical figures like the "blighted, ruined form" of the southern man and the brooding black mother; he draws upon the figures of contemporary intellectuals like Booker T. Washington, Alexander Crummell, and himself; and he attempts to create a narrative of the African American folk. I will discuss the gendered characteristics of the first two types of figuration at some length later, but first I wish to consider the way in which Du Bois genders his narrative of the folk.

The folk are first introduced in the fourth chapter, "Of the Meaning of Progress," in a narrative based upon Du Bois's memories of being a teacher in the rural district of Wilson County, Tennessee. Du Bois taught there for two consecutive summers, while he was a student at Fisk University, and he stayed with the Dowell family. One member of that family, a young woman, Josie Dowell, is transformed by Du Bois into a particularly interesting and memorable character whose life and death become a measure for the historical progress of the folk as a whole. Josie is the center of her family and essential to its survival. She harbors a "longing to know" and is the first student to enroll in Du Bois's school. Josie, in other words, becomes a symbol for the desires and the struggles of the African American folk, struggles which are epitomized by attempts to obtain an education. When Du Bois returns to visit the family ten years later—a passage of narrative time during which the liberal reader would expect to see evidence of progress and the fruition of Josie's desires—we learn abruptly that "Josie was dead" (p. 103). Josie's life and death become a metaphor for what progress has meant for the folk; her body is the ground upon which the contradictions between African American desires and ambition and the ambition and desires of white society are fought.[35]

The individual story of Josie is immediately followed by the collective narrative of Atlanta, a city Du Bois describes as a site of contradictions, lying "South of the North, yet North of the South" (p. 109). Atlanta is portrayed as embodying the desires and ambitions of the white world of the South, desires and ambitions that are founded on material greed. If Atlanta represents a possible future for the nation, it will be a future that grows from the outcome of the struggle for the "soul" of the black folk, Du Bois asserts. If that is so, it would seem to be a future built upon the literal and metaphoric deaths of all Josies.

In the fifth chapter, "Of the Wings of Atalanta," Du Bois personifies and genders the city as female and elevates it to the position of a central character in his narrative. He uses the myth of Atalanta and Hippomenes, in which Atalanta, who could outrun and outshoot any man with whom she came into competition, was betrayed by her own greed. Constantly chased by suitors, Atalanta declared that she would only marry the man who could beat her in a foot race, knowing that no one ran faster than she. Hippomenes decides that only guile can help him win, and during the course of his race with Atalanta rolls golden apples in her path, knowing that she will not be able to resist retrieving them. Atalanta falls to temptation and when she swerves to pick up the final apple loses the race to Hippomenes.

Du Bois's particular interpretation of this myth is sexually charged. He reflects that "Atalanta is not the first or last maiden whom greed of gold has led to defile the temple of love," and a greed for gold becomes entwined with a narrative of sexual lust, a mark that stains the city. "If Atlanta be not named for Atalanta, she ought to have been," he concludes (pp. 110–111).[36] In particular, Du Bois fears for "the black young Atalanta" who, instead of running a noble race to a glorious future, might stoop for the golden apples strewn by the American Mammon (p. 114).

At this point in the text we can see the gendered consequences of the order of the chapters. Atlanta, as a city embodying the gold-lust of Atalanta, is the center of the section that depicts a predominantly white world. The heart of first section of *The Souls of Black Folk*, then, is organized as a primarily female symbolic space dominated by the figures of Josie and the city of Atlanta. But even though the heart of the text at this point is female, this does not mean that concern with what is female is central to Du Bois's conceptual frame of reference. On the contrary, the metaphoric and symbolic characteristics of Josie and Atlanta determine that neither is a symbol of hope for the future of the African American folk, indeed neither have a viable political, social, or intellectual future in Du Bois's text. Although as a student at Fisk he was surrounded by black female intellectuals who were his peers, he was not yet able to imagine a community in which positive intellectual and social transformation could be evoked through female metaphors or tropes.[37]

Chapters seven and eight, in the middle of the book, begin to mark the transition from a predominantly white to a predominantly black world, a journey of descent into the black belt of the southern states and through an economic history of black emmiseration under a system of forced labor. This descent is not only into a black world but into a world of disappointed, embittered men who are also hopelessly in debt. The narrative exposes the reality of an apartheid system in housing, in economic relations, in political activity, and in the legal system. The white South is shown in utter spiritual as well as political turmoil, without a soul. The account of this turbulent white world is merely a coda, however, for a journey into the wholesome, spiritual, and soulful existence of black people in chapter ten, "Of the Faith of Our Fathers," which begins the final third of the book.

Within the opening pages of *The Souls of Black Folk*, Du Bois establishes his ability to speak as a race leader and grants himself the authority to evoke a convincing portrayal of the black folk by integrating his own commanding narrative voice, as a black intellectual, with the life of the folk, and his own body with his philosophy. From *Genesis* Du Bois takes the words of Adam and, transforming the pronouns, uses them to mark his own body as an essential part of that wider community his text imagines. "And, finally, need I add," he declares in the last sentence of his introduction, "that I who speak here am bone of the bone and flesh of the flesh of them that live within the veil" (p. xii). It was Du Bois's ambition to fashion a book that could create and make tangible the "soul" of a race in space and time, and he utilizes his own body to enable that soul to be imagined. Such embodiment is also an important trope to Cornel West:

> The Victorian three-piece suit—with a clock and a chain in the vest—worn by W. E. B. Du Bois not only represented the age that shaped and molded him; it also dignified his sense of intellectual vocation, a sense of rendering service by means of a critical intelligence and moral action. The shabby clothing worn by most black intellectuals these days may be seen as symbolizing their utter marginality behind the walls of academe and their sense of impotence in the wider world of American culture and politics.[38]

West's claim is that moral and ethical values of intellectual practice are inscribed in the clothed body, and these clothes secure the status of the intellect within. The clothes can then be read, unproblematically, as clear signs of intellectual worth [Illustrations I and II].

A comparison of the photographs of Du Bois and Cornel West demonstrates how the male body can be sculpted to model an intellectual mentor. But to define this appearance as the *only* acceptable confirmation of intellectual vocation, critical intelligence, and moral action is also to secure these qualities as irrevocably and conservatively masculine. Just as Du Bois constantly replaces and represses images of sexual desire (in his chapter on Atlanta) with evocations of a New England work ethic, so West equates the body and mind as disciplined and

I. W. E. B. Du Bois (ca. 1907)
Special Collections and Archives, W. E. B. Du Bois Library,
University of Massachusetts Amherst

contained within a dark, severely cut three-piece suit, buttoned shirt, and tightly drawn tie.

As the readers are gradually drawn into the center of the spiritual and cultural life of Du Bois's black folk, that life becomes increasingly African in its soul and masculine in its body. With the entry into the black world, the multiple narrative personae (historian, sociologist, and phi-

II. Cornel West (1993)
Courtesy Benno Friedman

losopher) are gradually stripped away. While the souls of black folk are to be revealed through religion and music, the heart and soul of the author are revealed through the grief of a father after the death of his son.

Chapter eleven, "Of the Passing of the First Born," is one of the most direct and passionate revelations of a male soul in American literature.[39] Children are commonly figured as embodiments of the hopes and fears of the previous generation, and this is how Du Bois represents his son.

As he does so, in his role of narrator Du Bois becomes a cypher, simply the transmitter of the frustrated dreams and fears of an entire people, the black folk.

> Within the veil was he born . . . and there within shall he live,—a Negro and a Negro's son. Holding in that little head—ah, bitterly!—the unbowed pride of a hunted race clinging . . . to a hope not hopeless but unhopeful, and seeing with those bright wondering eyes that peer into my soul a land whose freedom is to us a mockery and whose liberty is a lie. . . . I . . . saw the strength of my own arm stretched onward through the ages through the newer strength of his; saw the dream of my black fathers stagger a step onward in the wild phantasm of the world; heard in his baby voice the voice of the prophet that was to rise within the veil. (pp. 227–228)

Here Du Bois attempts to fuse his own body with a racialized way of knowing the world, "a Negro and a Negro's son . . . saw the dream of my black father." But he also situates himself as an intellectual and spiritual mediator between the world and his people and interpreter of the meanings of their dreams and fears for their collective future.

For Du Bois the contradictions and ambiguities of his genealogy of race and nation exist metaphorically within the boundaries of his own soul, in which a deep pessimism wars with an emergent sense of optimism about the future of black men within the national community. This struggle of and for the soul of a people, which is enacted within the soul of the narrator, culminates in a recognition that the loss of his son reveals the consequences of the sacrifice that Du Bois was willing, in the abstract, to make in 1893: "now there wails, on that dark shore within the veil, the . . . deep voice, *Thou Shalt Forego!* And all have I foregone at that command, and with small complaint,—all save that fair young form that lies so closely wed with death in the nest I had builded" (p. 232). The death of his son places the fate of the race, figuratively, back within the hands of Du Bois, a leader with no heir.

Du Bois's reflections on the life on Alexander Crummell, in the following chapter, lie in startling juxtaposition to the meanings he derives from the death of his son. The issue of who shall inherit the mantle of intellectual leadership is again the central question. Although Crummell lived long enough to become a man who gained the "voice of the prophet," this voice could not bring into being its own prophecies, for Crummell has no acolytes. Therefore Crummell's name remains unknown, despite his devoting his entire life to intellectual leadership. Here, again, Du Bois locates himself as the only remaining conduit for disseminating Crummell's work and principles among the race, and the only possible agent for translating those principles of leadership into action.

The story of "The Coming of John" elaborates these paradigms and continues to evoke tension and anxiety about a lack of a viable future for the race, as white and black male desires and hopes violently conflict and result in their mutual destruction. But in this essay Du Bois also consciously confronts and contradicts claims that white male aggression is met only by black male passivity—Black John actually kills his white childhood companion, also named John, for attempting to rape his sister. In this struggle over the control of female sexuality and sexual reproduction, John gains self-respect in his own black manhood. Although his bravery leads to his death, his manner of dying can be a model of manhood for future generations. Here again, the future of Du Bois's imagined black community is to be determined by the nature of the struggle among men over the bodies of women.

As an intellectual, Du Bois was obviously concerned about the continuity of intellectual generations, what I would call the reproduction of Race Men. This anxiety permeates and structures the essays on his son, on Alexander Crummell, and on the two Johns. The map of intellectual mentors he draws for us is a map of male production and reproduction that traces in its form, but displaces through its content, biological and sexual reproduction. It is reproduction without women, and is a final closure to Du Bois's claim to be "flesh of the flesh and bone of the bone," for in the usurpation of the birth of woman from Adam's rib, the figure of the intellectual and race leader is born of and engendered by other males.

This anxiety continues to be evoked in the work of contemporary black male intellectuals. In an eloquent and moving passage, Henry Louis Gates, Jr. gives an account of his generation at Yale: "Some of the black students I knew at Yale dropped out, or pursued militancy to a point of no return, or went mad." But the premature deaths of two who did not drop out, who could have become intellectuals and race leaders, leads him to mourn an even greater loss:

> It is also true that some of the black students I knew at Yale have gone on to serve in Congress, as big-city mayors, as presidents and vice-presidents of major conglomerates. This is what members of the crossover generation are supposed to do: cross over. This is what the civil activists and social engineers who recruited us had in mind. It's how the trope of the "Talented Tenth" was to be retrieved and refashioned for modern times. And yet there's a sense in which DeChabert and Robinson [who did not cross-over] represented more to me than any of the "success stories"; and their failures of fulfillment (the oldest college story of all) grieved and rankled me as my own. I didn't go to their funerals: the truth is, I wasn't ready for them to be dead, either of them. We were supposed to storm the citadel together, to summer at Martha's Vineyard together, to grow old together. They would be on hand to explain to me the difference between selling out and buying in. Our kids were supposed to marry each other; to graduate from schools where we would give the commencement addresses. Ours was to be the generation with cultural accountability, and cultural security: the generation that would tell white folks that we would not be deterred—that, whether they knew it or not, we too were of the elite.[40]

Gates's generational map, like that of Du Bois, is permeated by a particular anxiety of masculinity, an anxiety which is embedded in the landscape of a crisis in the social order. The particularity of the loss of men who are called by name, and grieved in part for the failure of intellectual reproduction, contrasts dramatically with the generality of the social crisis of poverty which he documents as reproduced through the figures of anonymous single mothers.[41]

Having considered the consequences of the narrative structure of *The Souls of Black Folk*, I want to consider its conceptual structure, drawn from Du Bois's creative interrelation of the complex meanings of race and nation. The individual essays that comprise *The Souls of Black Folk* are composed and tied to each other to form a series of tightly bound ideological contradictions, contradictions which are themselves inherent in the particularities of the racial ordering of the United States as a modern nation-state. The text exposes and exploits the tension that exists between the internal egalitarian impulse inherent in the concept of nation and the relations of domination and subordination that are embodied in a racially encoded social hierarchy.[42] Du Bois recognized that the question of the relation between nationalism and racism was a matter of understanding their historical articulation, and he therefore attempted to rewrite the historical as well as the sociological genealogy of black people, situating them as equal citizens within the national community.[43]

Du Bois did not contest the claim that black people should be viewed as a race. On the contrary, his intellectual strategy was to utilize the concept of race and transform it into a means of political unification. In *The Souls of Black Folk* he imagines black people as a race in ways that are conceptually analogous to imagining them as a nation. Processes of racialization are usually understood to be fragmentary in their historical effect on national political communities, and, indeed, *The Souls of Black Folk* was produced at a time when the nation was internally organized into a system of rigid racial segregation maintained and policed by the politics of terror. Adopting a strategy of direct confrontation with the historical conditions under which he wrote, Du Bois asserted that processes of racialization could create *unified* communities existing in harmony with the national community. He stated:

Work, culture, liberty,—all these we need, not singly but together, not successively but together, each growing and aiding each, and all striving toward that vaster ideal that swims before the Negro people, the ideal of human brotherhood, gained through the unifying ideal of Race; the ideal of fostering and developing the traits and talents of the Negro, not in opposition to or contempt for other races, but rather in large conformity to the great ideals of the American Republic. (p. 52)

Conceptual tension arises from the differing inflections of the concept of race in this passage. While Du Bois attempted to avoid the use of the term in the sense of the limited genetic concept which had historically condemned the descendants of African peoples in the United States to exclusion from the framework of national citizenship, he retained the metaphorical and familial language of racial kinship. At this point in his intellectual life, Du Bois used the concept of race to signify cultural difference (a designation now more frequently associated with the concept of ethnicity). He paid little attention to analyzing or criticizing actual material *processes* of racial categorization, and concentrated instead upon documenting the historical *effects* of racialization by focusing upon the historically constituted and conventional racialized *meanings* inscribed in the social and political constitution of blackness.[44]

In the opening chapter, "Of Our Spiritual Strivings," Du Bois challenges the dominant ideological definitions of the historical, sociological, and political position of black people within the boundaries of the national community. His initial philosophical premise is that black people and black cultural forms do not exist in opposition to the ideals of an American republic but, on the contrary, embody them. Consequently, instead of participating in the contestation over categories of racial differentiation, he locates the symbolic power of nationalism, of Americanness, squarely within the black cultural field.

We the darker ones come even now not altogether empty-handed: there are today no truer exponents of the pure human spirit of the

Declaration of Independence than the American Negroes; there is no true American music but the wild sweet melodies of the Negro slave; the American fairy tales and folklore are Indian and African; and, all in all, we black men seem the sole oasis of simple faith and reverence in a dusty desert of dollars and smartness. (p. 52)

The reference to the "pure human spirit of the Declaration of Independence" evokes "the pervasive *republicanism* of the newly-independent [national] communities" of the eighteenth century.[45] Claiming this particular genealogy for black peoples has very particular political and ideological effects. It is a demand for inclusion in the "imagined community" of the nation-state produced by the cultural revolutions of the modern world. This demand contrasts dramatically, for example, with the way in which Marcus Garvey would, in the coming years, structure the U.N.I.A., an organization ideologically and politically incompatible with the idea of a modern nation-state: a racialized fraternity, it was conceived in the terms of a premodern dynastic order.[46]

The Souls of Black Folk is organized and framed by the symbolic unification of race and nation, and in its closing pages Du Bois repeats his strategy of placing black bodies at the center of the national discourse. Black people, he asserts, are integral to the very formation and maintenance of the nation-state to which they have donated their particular gifts: "a gift of story and song—soft, stirring melody in an ill-harmonized and unmelodious land; the gift of sweat and brawn to beat back the wilderness, conquer the soil and lay the foundations of this vast economic empire two hundred years earlier than your weak hands could have done it; the third, a gift of the Spirit. . . . Actively we have woven ourselves with the very warp and woof of this nation" (p. 275).

In language simultaneously evocative of the history of the frontier and of the industrial cotton mills, Du Bois rejects the marginalization of black people in American national life, whom he sees as integral to the founding and formation of the republic. In *The Souls of Black Folk* it is the descendants of African peoples who are proclaimed the legitimate inheritors of the principles of the Declaration of Independence, and Du Bois inscribes the symbolic power of nationalism directly onto black bodies. It is the bodies of the previously enslaved which inherit, and therefore become the primary site for, the preservation of national ideals. It is black bodies which offer the only vision of spiritual sustenance in a desert of rampant materialism, and it is the conditions of *their* social, political, and economic existence, Du Bois asserts, which are the only reliable measure of the health of the national body politic. In the body of America dwells a black soul.

What is at stake for Du Bois is to convince his readership that what appear to be ideologically and historically oppositional categories, namely race and nation, are not, in fact, incompatible. Yet crucial to Du Bois's structure of thought is the way he uses gender to mediate the relation between his concept of race and his concept of nation. This enables him to negotiate his way between the contradictions of a nationalist discourse of equality, on the one hand, and a fragmentary and hierarchical discourse of race, on the other.[47] The process of gendering at work in *The Souls of Black Folk* distinguishes not only between concepts of masculine and feminine subject positions but makes distinctions within his definition of masculinity itself.

The multiplicity and complexity of Du Bois's intellectual project, which integrates the discourses of history, philosophy, and social science, is bound with the thread of an apparently unified gendered subject position. In "Of Our Spiritual Strivings," the title of the first chapter, the opening pages establish the "I" of an autobiographical narrator, an "I" that quickly links itself to the "Our," the black community, through the experience of being regarded as a problem. The basis for this shared experience, however—a racist social order—is the same ground which establishes the narrator as an exceptional male individual. Du Bois's intellectual and political intention to integrate *his* voice with the voice of the wider black community displaces a number of ideological contradictions, not the least of which is his class position. In order to retain his credentials for leadership, Du Bois had to situate himself as both an exceptional and a representative individual: to be different from and maintain a distance between his experience and that of the masses of black people, while simultaneously integrating his existential being with that of his imagined community of the people. The terms and conditions of his exceptionalism, Du Bois argues, have their source in his formation as a *gendered* intellectual.

The "striving" that was required in order to exist in a racist society was of a different order for Du Bois than for most black men, he states. As a schoolboy, he was able to beat his white classmates at examination time, and this success, he concludes, enabled him to overcome his contempt of them. Attributing to his success in school the source of his emotional maturity emphasizes Du Bois's intellectual ability and superiority. In this, however, his becoming a man differed from the way most other black boys grew to manhood. As Du Bois describes this distinction: "With other black boys the strife was not so fiercely sunny: their youth shrank into tasteless sychophancy, or into silent hatred of the pale world about them and mocking distrust of everything white; or wasted itself in a bitter cry, Why did God make me an outcast and a stranger in mine own house?" (pp. 44–45).[48] Du Bois's intellectual and sexual formation are twin aspects of the constitution of black masculinity, and their interdependence is manifest in the gendered language of his text.

For Du Bois the "problem" of being black was an issue of both commonality and exceptionalism; it was not just about learning that he was black but also about learning how to *become* a black man. The story of his first memorable racist incident is also the re-creation of a highly charged moment of gender formation. He describes how all his classmates decided to exchange visiting cards. A white girl arrogantly refused to accept the card Du Bois offered her and at that moment, he writes, he knew that he was "different" from his white peers and became aware of the "veil" that separated their two worlds. This realization disrupts the smooth passage of the formative years of his male adolescence, but the practice of challenging and overcoming such obstacles enables the transition from boy to man.[49]

The conceptual structure of Du Bois's genealogy of race and nation has, at its center, the dilemma of the formation of black manhood. Gender mediates Du Bois's presentation of the relation between race, nation, and a fully participatory citizenship for black people. Integral to the "problem" of simultaneously being black and being American is coming into manhood, and it is the latter that is the most vulnerable to attack. For racism shrank the youth of most black boys into a "tasteless sychophancy" which not only disrupts adolescence but dooms these young men to a life of mimicry, to a mere a parody of masculinity, a parody which results in their being denied a full role in the patriarchal social and political order.

Du Bois's characterization of a parody of masculinity echoes today in Cornel West's descriptions of the "nihilism" of black America, and in his analysis of the formation of black male sexuality. West makes a clear distinction between "black male sexuality" and "black female sexuality"; he argues, for instance, that "black men have different self-images and strategies of acquiring power in the patriarchal structures of white America and black communities. For most young black men, power is acquired by stylizing their bodies over space and time in such a way that their bodies reflect their uniqueness and provoke fear in others." West is convinced that it is these "limited stylistic options" which lead to their patriarchal subordination. This stylizing of bodies is "an instance of machismo," West insists, which "solicits primarily sexual encounters with women and violent encounters with other black men or aggressive police. . . . This search for power . . . usually results in a direct confrontation with the order-imposing authorities of the status quo, that is, the police or the criminal justice system."[50] West's argument about the style of young black men stands in direct contrast to his image of the successful black intellectual in a three-piece suit and is directly analogous to Du Bois's arguments about the deformation of the process of young black men becoming gendered beings at the turn of the century. What Du Bois regards as a black male style that is a parody of a national discourse of masculinity is equivalent to Cornel West's "machismo" style of young black men, which "solicits primarily sexual encounters with women and violent encounters with other black men" and brings them into direct confrontation with the authority of the nation-state.

It is significant that Du Bois claims that his first encounter with racism was the moment when his courtly, nineteenth-century advances were rejected by a young white woman. Du Bois clearly believed that women (and, I will argue, certain men whom he regarded as having compromised their masculinity) could become the mediators through which the nation-state oppressed black men. For most black men, he argues, the burden of racism was not only poverty and ignorance but a burden carried through black mothers and imposed upon their sons. "The red stain of bastardy, which two centuries of systematic legal defilement of Negro women had stamped upon his race," Du Bois concludes, fell upon the shoulders of black men, as they had to carry "the hereditary weight of a mass of corruption from white adulterers" (p. 50). This "hereditary weight" is the burden imposed on black men by history because they could not control the sexual reproduction of black women. Under this weight of betrayal by black women, most black men stumbled, fell, and failed to come into the full flowering of black manhood.

Most black men, in Du Bois's genealogy, suffer from a deformation in their process of becoming gendered beings; the result is their patriarchal subordination in the national community. Du Bois's language in *The Souls of Black Folk* is passionately gendered in its symbolic power as he describes such subordination. In addition to the weight that the black man had to bear because of the defilement of Negro women, Du Bois describes how the "shadow of the vast despair" that darkens "the very soul of the toiling, sweating black man" was made even more unbearable by white sociologists who "gleefully count his bastards and his prostitutes." For Du Bois the figure of the black woman, whether prostitute or mother, has a surplus symbolic value upon which he liberally draws in his illustrations of the denigration of the black man. The illicit sexuality that Du Bois inscribes upon the bodies of black women contributes to rendering the male impotent, so that the black man "stands helpless, dismayed and well-nigh speechless; before that personal disrespect and mockery, the ridicule and systematic humiliation, the distortion of fact and wanton license of fancy" (p. 50).

Although paralysis of mind and body is the fate of most black men, *The Souls of Black Folk* stands as evidence that Du Bois is an exception:[51]

he retains an ability to speak in a voice that has overcome the vast despair that defeats lesser men; he has lifted the burden of illegitimacy and female sexual complicity from his shoulders, and he has conquered the impotence caused by such a burden.[52] It is the process of becoming an intellectual that Du Bois offers as an alternative route to manhood, as a way to avoid gendered and racialized subordination, deformation, and degradation. Indeed, becoming an intellectual is, perhaps, the only sure route to becoming a certain type of man, a man whose "style" is not in direct confrontation with the nation-state. Du Bois insists that it is his *intellectual* achievements that enable him to make a successful transition from adolescence into a socially acceptable style of manhood, and that it is the power of his intellect which gives him the ability to analyze the burden, the vast shadow, which stunts and deforms the growth of other black men. The practice of intellectual analysis, as narratively encoded within *The Souls of Black Folk*, conquers political impotence and leads to an attainment of masculine self-respect. It is this theory of conquest by intellect that I would now like to consider.

In *The Souls of Black Folk* Du Bois not only challenges his readers to reconsider the ways in which the national community has been historically constituted, but he also creates an alternative cultural identity for the nation-state. Despite the apparent idealism of this project, Du Bois was certainly aware that even if he succeeded, neither the cultural recognition of the historic role of black people in the formation of the nation-state nor their inclusion in the nationalist symbolic order would automatically result in the granting of universal suffrage and political citizenship: acts which would signify their inclusion within the imagined boundaries of the nation-state. Thus it was essential for Du Bois to provide a framework for the future political praxis of black leadership.

Through a series of reflections Du Bois developed what he regarded as the necessary conditions for producing black political and intellectual leadership. In the sixth chapter, "Of the Training of Black Men," Du Bois appraises black education and argues for the importance of producing a college-educated elite, a "Talented Tenth" which would teach and provide leadership for the race. This "Talented Tenth," however, was not to remain an isolated intellectual elite but would evolve in alliance with its constituency, an alliance he describes as a "loving, reverent comradeship between the black lowly and the black men emancipated by training and culture" (p. 138). Black intellectuals are to become the means for inducting the "lowly" into the national community; as teachers, their role becomes that of missionaries for the nation-state.[53]

In the ninth chapter, "Of the Sons of Master and Man," Du Bois elaborates upon these ideas and insists that leaders who had assimilated "the culture and common sense of modern civilization" play an important role in imagining the "race" as part of the national entity, a role, I have argued, that Du Bois himself was effecting by bringing black people into the boundaries of the national imagination through *The Souls of Black Folk*. However, representing the race as part of the national entity bespoke the obligation to turn the representation into reality: in order to effect change those leaders needed access to political power. The ballot was recognized to be an important *mechanism* for the production of actual and symbolic national subjects but it was through the *practice* of exercising their right to vote that black men could imagine their own relation as subjects to a political community. In 1903, Du Bois regarded the ballot as perhaps the most important means for a black political and intellectual elite to acquire political power and signify black political citizenship.

The philosophy and practice of black intellectual leadership was to be bound by the same limits and commitments that Du Bois imposed upon himself in 1893. Although there are specific passages in *The Souls of Black Folk* where Du Bois discusses the present and future condition of black leadership in the abstract, and occasionally in relation to specific individuals such as Booker T. Washington and Alexander Crummell, the narrative is stitched together by an authorial persona who enacts the ideal qualities of intellectual and political leadership and black masculinity. Du Bois himself is textually present in three important ways: first, he acts as an embodiment of his own ideal of an intellectual and graduate of the humanistic education he advocates; second, he appears as a contestant for black leadership whose voice gains authority through the process of critiquing other male leaders; and, finally, he quite deliberately uses his own body as the site for an exposition of the qualities of black manhood.

In Du Bois's genealogy of race and nation, black people are both integral to the nation-state and essential to its future. An important political element of his blueprint for black intellectuals is the development and elaboration of a critique of rampant materialism. In a period which gives rise to the global expansion of capitalism and secures the rapid "incorporation" of the United States, black men are "the sole oasis of simple faith and reverence in a dusty desert of dollars and smartness" (p. 52).[54] In chapter five, "On the Wings of Atalanta," Du Bois elaborates this world view and places himself at its axis.

The chapter opens with his critique of materialism and fear that within the black world as well as the white, "the habit is forming of interpreting the world in dollars" (p. 113). The city of Atlanta, epitome of industrialization and material greed, is what gave birth to the new South, Du Bois asserts. He describes how "the city crowned her hundred hills with factories" (p. 110) and warns that "Atlanta must not lead the South to dream of material prosperity as the touchstone of all success" (p. 112). But in this "desert" bloomed Atlanta University, a world that was not obsessed with the dream of material prosperity and had a vision of life with "nothing mean or selfish" in it.

Not at Oxford or at Leipsic, not at Yale or Columbia, is there an air of higher resolve or more unfettered striving; the determination to realize for men, both black and white, the broadest possibilities of life, to seek the better and the best, to spread with their own hands the Gospel of Sacrifice,—all this is the burden of their talk and dream. Here, amid a wide desert of cast and proscription, amid the heart-hurting slights and jars and vagaries of a deep race-dislike, lies this green oasis. (pp. 115–116)

Using the language of sacrifice and commitment which in 1893 he had confined to his personal diary, Du Bois creates an image of the

University of Atlanta as a body politic which could be the source of alternative humanistic values and ideals and, at the heart of it, putting the "air of higher resolve" and "unfettered striving" into practice, Du Bois places himself.

The language and narrative structure of *The Souls of Black Folk* define the university as being at once the foundation of a civilization under threat and, through its production of professional intellectuals, the promise of a new social order for the nation. As Eric Hobsbawn put it, "the progress of schools and universities measures that of nationalism just as schools and universities become its most conscious champions."[55] By explicitly situating himself as speaking from the University of Atlanta, Du Bois establishes himself as a professional intellectual in a position of authority from which he could, as an intellectual and as a critic of culture, intervene in and shape debate about the boundaries of culture and civilization, broadening its parameters to imaginatively include black men and black folk culture.

But the professional intellectual needs not only a site from which to speak but a "true self-consciousness" to determine what is spoken. The concept of double-consciousness is generally regarded as one of Du Bois's major contributions to philosophic thought. Explicated in the first chapter of *The Souls of Black Folk*, double-consciousness is the product of a world that has allowed the black man no "true self-consciousness but only lets him see himself through the revelation of the other world" (p. 45). While double-consciousness is, indeed, a product of the articulation between race and nation, I would argue that we need to revise our understanding of how this double-consciousness works in order to understand how gender is an ever-present, though unacknowledged, factor in this theory. For Du Bois, the gaining of the "true self-consciousness" of a racialized and national subject position is dependent upon first gaining a gendered self-consciousness.

In order to explicate this assertion I want to return to the second chapter, "Of the Dawn of Freedom," and its two contrasting figures which typify the gendered nature of the history of Reconstruction. Each figure is imagined to bear the history of its race in the South. The first one is white: "a grey-haired gentleman" who, although "his fathers had quit themselves like men," is unable to father future generations or leave a legacy of patriarchal power because his sons "lay in nameless graves." This figure is an unmanned and "blighted, ruined form, with hate in his eyes." The second figure is black: a mother with an "awful face" who "quailed at that white master's command," loved his sons and his wife, and "laid herself low to his lust." Her legacy is a "tawny manchild" born out of an act of submission—an act of racial betrayal which compromises the black man's masculinity because it does not recognize his control over her sexual being.

Two acts of compromise, one political and one sexual, lead to the perpetual subordination of black manhood. The act of sexual compromise by Du Bois's anonymous figure of the black mother, which contributes to the black man's failure to become a man, is deliberately situated in the narrative of Reconstruction so as to parallel the Act of Compromise of 1877 between the northern and southern states, an act which put an end to the work of the Freedmen's Bureau, led to the withdrawal of northern troops from the South, and resulted in further oppression of black men. Each act of compromise renders the nation impotent, unable and unwilling to fully emancipate the black man. "For this much all men know" wrote Du Bois, "despite compromise, war and struggle, the Negro is not free" (p. 77). The integrity and the autonomy of race, of nation, and of masculinity are destroyed by such acts of compromise in which the sexual and political subordination of black manhood are figuratively intertwined.

The gendered nature of the language in chapter three, "Of Mr. Booker T. Washington and Others," continues to allude to the sexual compromise evoked by Du Bois's figure of the black mother. The "most notable thing in Mr. Washington's career," Du Bois states with undisguised irony, is his "Atlanta Compromise" (p. 80). Washington's body becomes a spectacle set against the landscape described as a "dusty desert of dollars and smartness." Initially, Du Bois characterizes Washington as a sycophant and as destructive as the materialistic idols in front of which he prostrates himself. In a bitter tone he writes of him:

"And so thoroughly did [Washington] learn the speech and thought of triumphant commercialism, and the ideals of commercial prosperity, that the picture of a lone black boy pouring over a French grammar amid the weeds and dirt of a neglected home soon seemed to him the acme of absurdities" (p. 81). Sycophancy and selling out to commercialism are cited as evidence of a stunted or deformed manhood, a masculine style incompatible with the incorporation of the race into the modern nation-state. Because Du Bois makes his narrative of the transition from male adolescence and immaturity to full manhood and maturity so entirely dependent upon becoming an intellectual, Washington's standing as an intellectual and as a race leader is challenged at the same time as his masculinity is undermined.

Du Bois deliberately constructs his figure of Washington as analogous to that of his anonymous black mother: both betray the sons of the race, both undermine the possibility of black patriarchal power, and both of their acts of submission are condemned with equal vehemence. When Washington mimics the speech and ideals of commercialism, he becomes the metaphorical equivalent of the black mother (or the black female prostitute) who succumbs to the lust of white men. Washington also stands accused of succumbing to the lust of his historical moment: his "oneness with his age" is ironically described as "the mark of a successful man" (p. 81), but his "counsels of submission," Du Bois concludes, "overlooked certain elements of true manhood" (p. 82). Not only is the reader left in little doubt that Washington is not a man by Du Bois's measure of black masculinity, but his compromise with the dominant philosophy of his age is to be understood as a form of prostitution.

The chapter on Booker T. Washington immediately precedes the two chapters that I describe as the female symbolic space of the white section of the book. The discussion of Washington is, therefore, separated and excluded from the black masculine world with which the text concludes, and juxtaposed with a feminized symbolic territory of illegitimate and negative sexuality. The city of Atlanta—whether evoked through Washington's "Atlanta Compromise" speech or as the symbolic landscape of commercial degradation in *The Souls of Black Folk*—is a female entity, historically compromised and starkly contrasted to the modern nation evoked as "this common Fatherland" (p. 91).

Du Bois's gendered language grows increasingly complex and sexually explicit when he considers the future of the Union. "We have no right," he says, "to sit silently by while the inevitable seeds are sown for a harvest of disaster to our children, black and white" (p. 92). Washington is situated at the crux of two illegitimate symbolic sexual unions: he prostituted himself because he sold his soul and betrayed the best interests of black men; and he promoted the national reconciliation of the (female) South and "her co-partner in guilt," the North (p. 94).

Du Bois contrasts Washington's inadequate manliness and consequent lack of the attributes of leadership with a history of black male revolt and self-assertion led by such revolutionary figures as the maroons, Toussaint L'Ouverture, Nat Turner, and other rebels against Washington's acts of compromise. The heirs of these revolutionaries, Du Bois argues, are leaders like David Walker, Frederick Douglass and William Wells Brown—a list that excludes Washington but is the genealogy of the progenitors of Du Bois. These revolutionary figures appear in Du Bois's narrative both as "true" black men and genuine leaders of black men.

Washington, in contrast, figures as the equivalent of the bastard child: "Booker T. Washington arose as essentially the leader not of one race but of two—a compromiser between the South, the North and the Negro" (p. 86). He is twice a compromiser, a man who prostrates himself to whites and black alike and is himself a product of a national compromise. Washington's compromise, declares Du Bois, surrendered the civil and political rights of black men in the same way that the compromise between the North and the South betrayed these rights. Washington's policy of submission withdrew "many of the high demands of Negroes as men and as American citizens" (p. 87). His policies were "bound to sap the manhood of any race" (p. 88). They directly undermine the genealogy of race and nation Du Bois constructs in *The Souls of Black Folk*, just as the historical compromise between the northern and southern states undermines his political and philosophical ideals. In short, *The Souls of Black Folk* effectively dethrones Booker T. Washington from his position as a pre-eminent leader, questions his political and intellectual integrity, and condemns him as a collaborator.

The complex cultural politics of gender at work in *The Souls of Black Folk* are an important means of producing political displacement. The narrative demise of Booker T. Washington, of course, significantly advances Du Bois's own claim to speak with the authority of a representative black intellectual, leader, and man. But we should ask, at what cost has this figure of the representative black intellectual been produced? and to what extent do we still live with the politics of gender implicated in its production?

Do you think I could walk pleasantly
and well-suited toward annihilation?
with a scrotal sack full
of primordial loneliness
swinging between my legs
like solid bells?

ESSEX HEMPHILL

2

THE BODY AND
SOUL OF
MODERNISM

If ideologies of gender shape the structures of thought and feeling in the work of black male intellectuals, the politics of gender are also at work in representations of particular black male bodies. In this chapter I will focus on modernist evocations of race, nation, and manhood as these were inscribed upon the body of Paul Robeson during the 1920s and 1930s.

In *The Souls of Black Folk*, Du Bois's initial premise was that black people and black cultural forms did not exist in opposition to the national ideals but, on the contrary, embodied those ideals. He thus attempted to rewrite the dominant cultural and political script by transferring the symbolic power of nationalism, of Americanness, into a black cultural field and onto the black male body. Mediating his concepts of race and nation, I argued, is the concept of gender, woven into a complex philosophical discourse which sought to resolve anxieties about the formation of black intellectual manhood.

I suggest that the process of imaginatively incorporating black cultural forms into the national cultural community through the figure of the black male produces a number of significant cultural and political contradictions. Modernist representations and imaginings of the black male body within the framework of the national body politic have produced social and political meanings fraught with gendered anxieties and tensions.

What must always be remembered, I would stress, is that alongside the white fascination with primitivism[1] and the various cultural excavations to recover and claim an essence of masculinity, often believed to have been lost in the modern industrializing world, existed the imaginary fears and desires acted out in ritual fervor on the actual bodies of black men.

In 1917, James Weldon Johnson, acting in his capacity as Field Secretary for the National Association for the Advancement of Colored People (N.A.A.C.P.), went to Memphis to investigate the lynching of Ell Persons. As he stood on the spot where Ell Persons had been burnt alive, he mused:

A pile of ashes and pieces of charred wood still marked the spot. While the ashes were yet hot, the bones had been scrambled for as souvenirs by the mobs. I reassembled the picture in my mind: a lone Negro in the hands of his accusers, who for the time are no longer human; he is chained to a stake, wood is piled under and around him, and five thousand men and women, women with babies in their arms and women with babies in their wombs, look on with pitiless anticipation, with sadistic satisfaction while he is baptized with gasoline and set afire. The mob disperses, many of them complaining, "They burned him too fast." I tried to balance the sufferings of the miserable victim against the moral degradation of Memphis, and the truth flashed over me that in large measure the race question involves the saving of black America's body and white America's soul.[2]

As Johnson stands over the charred remains of just one of many thousands of black men and women lynched between the 1880s and 1940s, his reflections improvise upon, elaborate, and extend the multiple meanings of Du Bois's declaration that "the problem of the Twentieth Century is the problem of the color line."[3] The brutal public torture and dismemberment of blacks by white men, women, and children, enacted in the celebratory manner of participants at a rural county fair, must be recognized as the ever-present underside of artistic or philosophical imaginings of black masculinity as tropes of utopian possibility. We must ask if the ritual of dismemberment and sadistic torture of black bodies is, in fact, a search to expose, and perhaps even an attempt to claim, an essence of manhood that is both feared and desired, an essence of the possible which escapes its pursuers as the blood pours from their hands and soaks the earth.[4] Is the politics of terror absolutely integral to the politics of the modernist liberal imagination?[5]

Johnson situates the black male body at the center of what he perceives as a national crisis, a crisis conceived in the dual terms of black body and white soul. The duality, yet interdependence, of the terms "body" and "soul" is an appropriate figure for the relation between ideologies of gender and processes of racialization and nation-building as they are evoked in modernist cultural movements in the early decades of this century.

Gail Bederman, in *Manliness and Civilization*, has provided an eloquent and persuasive account of the interdependent relation between notions of manliness, conceptions of race, and ideas of civilization and civilized behavior and values, from the late nineteenth through the early years of the twentieth century.[6] Bederman traces a historical transition from the dominance of Victorian ideologies of manliness to the increasing use of discourses of masculinity. I would add to Bederman's insights, however, an insistence that within the framework of modernist cultural texts, the generalities of reference to a discourse of civilization are replaced by the specificities of reference to national belonging, as both black and white intellectuals and cultural producers increasingly represented the fate of the nation and black people as interdependent. As Johnson put it: "If the Negro is made to fail, America fails with him."[7]

To illustrate this interdependency I have chosen a series of modernist evocations of race, nation, and masculinity that were inscribed upon the figure of Paul Robeson. In the 1940s Robeson became such a nationally vilified figure, because of his unwavering commitment to socialism, that it is easy to forget that he had once been a national icon. Concentrating upon his early career, from the twenties through the late thirties, I will discuss the emergence of Robeson's multiple public images: as a stage and screen actor, as a college athlete, and as a singer of folk songs and spirituals. Each one can be seen as a particular modernist cultural artifact of imagination and longing, which attempts to establish a relation between the African American male body and the state of the national soul.

In a 1926 issue of the *New Republic,* Elizabeth Shepley Sergeant declared that

> Paul Robeson is not merely an actor and a singer of Negro Spirituals but a symbol. A sort of sublimation of what the Negro may be in the Golden Age hangs about him, and imparts to his appearances an atmosphere of affection and delight that is seldom felt in an American audience. . . . Six feet two and one-half inches tall, twenty-seven years old, black as the Ace of Spades, he is a man of outstanding gifts and of noble physical strength and beauty. His figure on the slave block, in *The Emperor Jones,* is remembered like a bronze of ancient mold.[8]

It is important to note what is being valorized in this paean to Robeson. While W. E. B. Du Bois argued that the significance of the spirituals lay in their evocation of a history of communal struggle against oppression, this insight is ignored by Sergeant. She claims for Robeson a transcendent and individual ideal of nobility and spiritual beauty removed from and actively repressing that history. Hers is a modernist invention, one among the variety of modernist molds of Robeson into which visions of his body were poured, and which produced a series of cultural imaginings that culminated in his elevation into the status of national icon. By becoming a black national symbol of masculinity,

Robeson combined, in uneasy stasis and for a brief period of time, the historically contradictory elements of race, nation, and masculinity.

Modernists are often thought to have been obsessed by the tensions, anxieties, and contradictory desires of the modern age, and the modernists' cultural texts, both critical and performative, have come to be seen as the public arena on which these conflicts were staged. If the desires of white modernists for an unambiguous, essential masculinity were to be located in a black body, then that representation had to resolve and surmount the social contradictions of North American racial history. An alternative and linear history was projected onto the body of Paul Robeson, a history that established links both to a classical past and to the possibilities of a utopian future. To quote Sergeant again:

> Unlike most moderns, Paul Robeson is not half a dozen men in one torn and striving body. The sureness of essential being takes him across the concert stage, as it did across the football field, with the fine, free movement of his strong athletic body, which is the reflection in action of an inward goal. Paul Robeson knows where he is bound. . . . The singer's negroid features are more marked on stage than off. His nose becomes a triangle of whiteness, his eyes white moons, his skin takes the milky lights that turn black into bronze. He has never seen a Georgia road gang but when he sings *Water Boy* the very accent and spirit of the Negro laborers enter into him. . . . Yet I have never seen on the stage a more civilized, a more finished and accomplished artistic gesture than his nod to his accompanist, the signal to begin the song. This gesture is the final seal of Paul Robeson's personal ease in the world. Even a Southerner would have difficulty in negating its quality and elbowing its creator from a sidewalk.[9]

I quote this passage at length for it contains the basic themes and elements that were forged into the many representations of Robeson as a national icon.

The physics of Robeson's image were blended and mixed in stages. In her essay Sergeant creates an internal, essential being which, she maintains, can be evoked from the surface and movement of Robeson's body, a body which she, herself, forges as she tempers, mutes, and sculpts his "blackness" into bronze. The social meanings of this "Negroness" were, thus, externally imposed interpretations, cultural imaginings produced from the surface of his body onto which was grafted a psychological reality. To modernist imaginings, Paul Robeson offered the possibility of unity for a fractious age, while he simultaneously embodied what the dominant social order imagined to be an essential "blackness" or "Negroness." Through this alchemy of the elements of classicism, a utopian representation of Robeson's body evolves as a prescription for the healing of the historical rupture of the nation between North and South. The cultural projection of meanings onto Robeson potentially applied to all black men because he was also represented as a symbol: "A sort of sublimation of what the Negro may be in the Golden Age"; or as an embodiment of "the very accent and spirit of . . . Negro laborers."

The wholeness of Robeson's essential black being, what Sergeant described as being "one, and clear cut, in the Greek or primitive sense," was one of the elements that Nickolas Muray sought to project in his photographs of Paul Robeson taken in 1925. An émigré from Hungary, a dance critic, a national and international champion swordsman, Muray was a celebrity portrait photographer whose work was published in many New York magazines, including *Harper's Bazaar* and *Vanity Fair*. His Greenwich Village studio, established in 1920, quickly became a locus of modernist New York social life and sensibility.[10] Muray's studies of Robeson were among many celebrity portraits the photographer made in the twenties, some of which were later gathered into the collection *The Revealing Eye*, but they are also an important subgenre of Muray's portraiture, his studies of nudes. What makes the Robeson photographs particularly unusual is that nude studies of the black male body were so rare in this period.[11]

Muray made extensive notes on his photographic sessions and, although none pertaining directly to the sittings with Robeson are to be found within his papers, his notes on other sessions reveal much about

Muray's method and style of work, his analytic mind and his philosophy, in short, his craft, and I will draw upon them in my readings of the Robeson studies. From the few nude studies that are mentioned in the notes it is clear that Muray was primarily interested in the nude bodies of dancers or the bodies of those he characterized as "athletic."

> Dancing is a form of serious and meticulous exercise, it develops one's body in the most beautiful sculpturesque manner. I've always been interested in sculpture and this was the nearest thing to express my feeling for line and expression of the body. It was not very difficult to convince some of the dancers to pose for me in the nude. This has given me a priceless collection looking back forty odd years of these famous names, preserving in picture form their fantastically beautiful bodies. Leonardo da Vinci had no such chance as I have had, nor could he have had better models for his work. . . .
>
> I studied all the Greek [word "Greek" crossed out and "great" substituted for it] great sculptors or painters—figure drawings or figure paintings—from the Renaissance down to the present generation. Your mind becomes a catalogue when you've recorded in its proper pigeon-holes, and it always comes out at the right moment when you want to do this thing.[12]

Clearly proud of his own athletic prowess,[13] Muray was fascinated by the athletic bodies of other men. In the notes of his photographic session with Bernarr Macfadden, publisher of the magazines *Dance*, *Physical Culture*, and *True Story*, whom he described, disparagingly, as "a little man" with "the psyche of a giant," Muray reported reassuring his subject: "You don't have to be shy, Mr. MacFadden.(sic) Just be yourself, as if you were all by yourself, all alone. I'm just non-existent, a piece of apparatus who is going to record your beautiful body."[14]

Yet in recording a series of photo sessions with Eugene O'Neill, commissioned by *Vanity Fair* in 1925, which took place on Cape Cod, in Bermuda, and in Muray's studio, the photographer seems to have had second thoughts about the use of the word "beautiful" to describe a body that he clearly did find beautiful and substituted the word "athletic" instead.[15]

Muray's nude photographs of Paul Robeson are in the tradition of the "Akademien," taken in a "simply furnished studio" in which "to portray immaculate, ideal, art-worthy, naked bodies."[16] As Peter Weiermair explains, "'Akademien' were published not only for art students but also for the broader public, which was mainly interested in the erotic content . . . art and physical training," and they "served as excuses for the reproduction of male nudes and as means of avoiding censorship in the mails."[17] Much as the claim of artistic merit might have been used as an excuse, it is also a claim that serves to displace eroticism, a process Weiermair calls the "alibi of camouflage." Allen Ellenzweig argues that this device also helped the circulation of studies of nudes outside of the circuit of high culture: "In photography's first half-century . . . there proved to be an audience for the male nude. . . . Yet when the male nude of the academies . . . found its larger public, a veil of antiquity was used to de-eroticize it."[18]

Muray's references to Leonardo da Vinci, to a tradition of classical sculpture, and to himself as a sculptor not only hark back to his early work as engraver but, more importantly, reinforce his claim to create authentic art, confirming the superiority of his "flesh-molding" to that of Bernarr Macfadden, for example, whom Muray regarded as a mere purveyor of the body to the masses through his popular *Physical Culture* magazine. Muray understood the contradictions at work in the relation between art and eroticism and strove to establish his own cultural "alibi" through a system of references to classicism and athleticism. Yet this "alibi" is complicated by the cultural and political meanings embedded in Robeson's "blackness."

In the photograph of Robeson printed in *The Revealing Eye* (1967) and *Muray's Celebrity Portraits* (1978)[19] [Illustration III], both the plain walled background and Robeson's skin have a dark grainy quality to them. What distinguishes Robeson's body from the surface of the wall behind him and makes him stand out from the background of the pho-

III. "Paul Robeson" (1925), by Nickolas Muray
Courtesy George Eastman House

tograph is a hard outline which gives the effect of an engraved or sculpted body.[20] Robeson is kneeling, his toes curled under to balance his torso, which is bent forward and turned toward the camera. His fists are clenched as if struggling to pull apart wrists that are manacled together. The strength in the fists is evident, but the chains are imaginary.

Robeson's chin, neck, and eyes are in deep shadow while the profile of his nose, eyebrow, upper cheek-bone, forehead, and lower lip are highlighted, with the result that his features are recognizable while his facial expression remains unfathomable. The space occupied by the body is compact and yet the body itself is molded by light and shadow in such a way as to imply a reservoir of great strength held in temporary reserve. His muscles are flexed and his shoulders, upper chest, right pectorals and biceps, front of thighs and back of calf muscles are highlighted, while his lower chest, abdomen, and inner thighs disappear into a triangle of deep shadow. Though the body is in repose, the tense muscles, the enlarged veins of the right arm and hand, and the light playing on his heels and curled toes indicate that, at any moment, this man could spring into action and become a force that could not be contained. The right forearm obscures the genital area, but the combination of the crossed arms and shadow, deepening down into the abdomen, actually creates the shape of a V that directs the viewer's gaze into the dark mysterious depths at the center of the body. Is this where Muray thought the essence of Robeson's black male self lay, in the deep shadows he himself creates? Is Muray's apparently sympathetic, modernist representation of Robeson's body ideologically related to the lynch mobs who ripped the genitals from their victims, as if they could literally lay claim to and destroy what they supposed was the black male essence?

The mood of the photograph is heavy, as if a great burden lay in the heart of its subject, and yet each highlighted muscle implies that deep emotion simmers just under the surface of the skin, an anger contained, restrained as much by the psychological binding of imagined chains as by the historical force of physical repression.

IV. "An Ethiopian Chief" (ca. 1896), by F. Holland Day
The Metropolitan Museum of Art, Alfred Stieglitz Collection, 1933
(33.43.157).

The eroticism of the photograph, particularly as it is produced through light and shadow sculpting the body and enhancing the textures of the skin, is reminiscent of the work of F. Holland Day.[21] In particular this photograph reproduces the erotic triangle of sexual promise of Holland Day's "An Ethiopian Chief" [Illustration IV]. Day used his chauffeur and servant, Alfred Tanneyhill, as the model for a series of "Nubian" portraits taken in 1897. These photographs, part of Day's homoerotic studies, are stylistically distinct from his portraits of white male nudes in the ways in which they use light and shadow to flesh-mold. In "An Ethiopian Chief" Day uses the material of the robe to enhance the picture's sexual promise, an effect that Muray copied in his photograph through his positioning of Robeson's arms. But Muray must also have been familiar with Day's other photographs of Tanneyhill, including "The Smoker" and "An Ethiopian Chief [or Menelek]" [Illustrations V and VI].

Muray believed that the most important assignment of a photographer was to produce "naturalness." "It's the photographer's job," he stressed, "to make the sitter un-self-conscious, relaxed or interested, serious or amused, and at the same time create a composition as he goes along that is attractive and artistic and natural."[22] He sought to achieve this "naturalness" by adopting the look of classical references of the Akademien. Other poses [Illustrations VII, VIII, and IX] utilize blocks to emphasize heroic strength, manipulating light and shadow to sculpt Robeson's muscles into Athenian aesthetics of masculine beauty, and not one allows him to gaze back at the camera/viewer.

If, as Allen Ellenzweig has argued, "the male gaze upon other men . . . is intrinsic to the medium [of photography] and its struggle to gain acceptance as an art form . . . [and] has called upon the most honored traditions of the Athenian Golden Age . . . to give credence to its own preliminary forays into the study of the nude," then how do we characterize the nature of Muray's gaze?[23] I would argue that the gaze is homoerotic, despite its air of classicism and athleticism, though I do not intend to conflate homoeroticism with homosexuality.[24] The masculine body is presented as a modernist ideal to be desired by other men, a standard for social ideals of masculinity, and a means for bringing to account the masculinity of the male viewer. Muray claims this modernist ideal is "natural," but the process of recognition and of desire for an ideal works only one way—the black subject is not allowed to gaze back at the viewer.[25] His photographs of Robeson do not promote a democratic or egalitarian ideal. In what they do not say, in their silences, their absences, and in what they repress, a history of exploitation and oppression, they reproduce the unequal relation of power and subjection of their historical moment. The expression of desire is not that of the black

V. "The Smoker" (1897), by F. Holland Day
The Metropolitan Museum of Art, Alfred Stieglitz Collection, 1933
(33.43.366).

VI. "An Ethiopian Chief [or Menelek]" (ca 1896), by F. Holland Day
The Metropolitan Museum of Art, Alfred Stieglitz Collection, 1933
(33.43.158). All rights reserved, The Metropolitan Museum of Art.

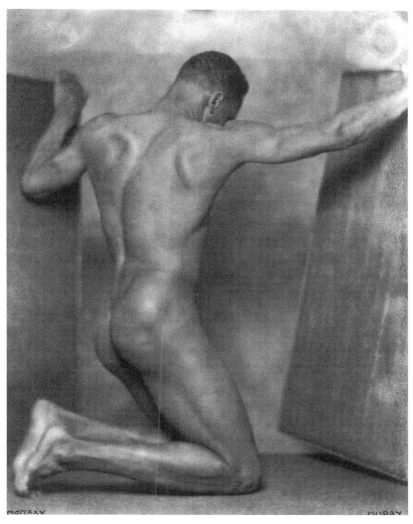

VII. "Paul Robeson" (1925), by Nickolas Muray
The Yale Collection of American Literature, Beinecke Rare Book and
Manuscript Library, Yale University

VIII. "Paul Robeson" (1925), by Nickolas Muray
The Yale Collection of American Literature, Beinecke Rare Book and
Manuscript Library, Yale University

IX. "Paul Robeson" (1925), by Nickolas Muray
The Yale Collection of American Literature, Beinecke Rare Book and
Manuscript Library, Yale University

subject for ultimate historical justice, but of the selfish longing of the modernist for an ideal.

To substantiate this argument further, consider another nude study, "Ethiopian Form," by Paul Outerbridge, Jr. [Illustration X].[26] Again, no power is granted to the subject to recognize the viewer, and the idealized physique exists only for consumption and to satisfy the desires of the viewer. Like Muray, Outerbridge creates an atmosphere of silent strength that could be aroused, but the potential of arousal is part of an erotic fantasy of power and lack of power. The eroticization and pleasure in creating and reproducing the potential of power is brought into being by the craft of the photographer, but it is also contained by that same craft, as the subject is restrained in the position of the abject. The act of containment recognizes the historical threat of black anger and rebellion, as it also renders it safe for consumption, a mold that satisfies and rewards the creator and those who share the standpoint of his gaze.[27]

Dorothy Donnell, in *The New Art of Camera Painting*, pointed out another feature of the craft:

Nickolas Muray is more than an expert mechanician of the camera. He is an artist. He sees people in the terms of pictorial compositions. He knows the inestimable value of shadows and uses them to produce miracles of flesh modelling. He possesses, moreover, a peculiarly keen power to analyze personalities and to transfer to paper, not only the features, but the very self of his sitters. . . .

He had a vision of photographs that would show, not a single individual, but humanity itself in all its human worth and dignity.[28]

Paul Gallico has also emphasized the significance of the photographer's psychological interpretation: "Muray's absorption with the personalities of the sitters was such that he practically resented the photographic apparatus as an interference. . . . [He] had his own way of breaking through, for unlike many artists whose lives are grimly wrapped up in

X. "Ethiopian Form" (ca. 1923), by Paul Outerbridge
Courtesy G. Ray Hawkins Gallery, Santa Monica. Copyright
© G. Ray Hawkins Gallery, Santa Monica

their work, he was a gay, laughing, cultured fellow and a psychologist as well . . ."[29]

Muray self-consciously employed a variety of stylistic, figurative, and metaphoric devices in his celebrity portraits to avoid what he considered to be merely "copying a person's outward physiognomy" and to present instead "the mood, the character, the intelligence, the beauty, the affectionate front which is known to friends, the family . . . publisher, manager, the editor who gives you assignments." It was important, wrote Muray, to have an "analytic mind" and "a philosophy" in order to show "the characteristics not only in front but what goes on behind the face."[30] To this end he selectively and creatively imposed a series of editorial and photographic decisions upon his subjects. As Alan Trachtenberg wrote: "Art, then, stands revealed as consisting of craft and the communication of knowledge."[31] It is this "flesh modelling," the process Muray and other modernists understood as revealing the "truth" of their subjects, that I regard as their most persuasive artistic fiction.

If the photographs of Robeson reveal what Muray regarded as Robeson's inner essence, his natural state of being, there are other conclusions we can draw from the decision to unclothe Robeson's body. In most of Muray's photographs clothes in general, and costumes in particular, are used, in addition to various props, to reveal to the viewer what he regards as the inner self or essential characteristics of his sitter. Thus writers, actors, singers—all of which are personae that Robeson also inhabited—are photographed in ways that emphasize the intellectual and artistic selves of these sitters, who gaze confidently back at the camera. Muray himself was photographed in his fencing uniform by Edward Steichen.

In contrast to Muray's photographic representations, the photograph Robeson chose as a gift for Carl Van Vechten was a portrait of himself as an intellectual, thoughtful and contemplative [Illustration XI]. In a suit and tie, Robeson sits with his face to the camera, eyes looking slightly toward the left. He is front-lit, with no shadows to indicate frowns, furrows, or creases on his forehead. One arm rests casually on the back of a wooden chair and another at his side, with his hand lying on his lap.

XI. Paul Robeson; photo was a gift to Carl Van Vechten
Courtesy of Joseph Solomon, Executor of the Estate of Carl Van Vechten.
The Yale Collection of American Literature, Beinecke Rare Book and
Manuscript Library, Yale University.

This was the persona that Robeson himself thought appropriate to present to the public. The mood is not only contemplative but peaceful. The photograph speaks of a man of convictions, a man who is at peace and who can speak for himself. The studio lighting suggests no violent inward emotions waiting to explode, or signs of an imminent eruption of violence.

In his study of the modernist Wyndham Lewis, Fredric Jameson asserts that "The most influential formal impulses of canonical modernism have been strategies of inwardness, which set out to reappropriate an alienated universe by transforming it into personal styles and private languages: such wills to style have seemed in retrospect to reconfirm the very privatization and fragmentation of social life against which they were meant to protest."[32] We can see these "strategies of inwardness" being evoked through representations of Robeson as embodying the wholeness that modern life lacked.

The conviction that issues of racial formation could be most effectively exposed through psychological dissection is the dominant characteristic of Kenneth Macpherson's film *Borderline*, in which both Paul and Essie Robeson appeared. As writer, producer, and director, Macpherson worked on the production of *Borderline* for a year, but the Robesons were filmed in only one week.[33] *Borderline* was one of a few film projects made by a small production company called Pool, and was the result of a collaboration between Kenneth Macpherson, Bryher, and H.D.[34] The modernist paradigm of body and soul structures the draft of a publicity notice written by its creators.

The border, or rather the line of the border, whose is it? . . . In this biological ground—biological and moral, or biological or moral— we have 'BORDERLINE': a negro couple in a white country, a couple that were separated, for she lived with a white man. . . . The drama between the white couple and the negro couple. The whites are neuroses; the negroes, nature. Nature turns to nature: Adah, the black woman, who had lived with the white couple Astrid and Thorne, abandons the latter to return to her husband Pete. But peace does not return; quite the reverse, for Thorne, exasperated by Adah's leaving him, and by the neurosis of Astrid, kills the latter. Adah, as a consequence of all this, disappears; and Pete, negro among whites, is expelled as undesirable.[35]

Macpherson's modernist aesthetic has some formal elements in common with Muray's camera work. Macpherson was a painter influenced by his father, a portrait painter, and his intention was that "each scene is a picture and each character has the force of a portrait."[36]

H.D. argued that Macpherson literally sculpted with light: "He gouges, he reveals, he conceals." She believed that in directing he was bringing "all these high powered vibrations of post static art into direct line with modern problems, with modernity and with the most modern out of portraiture in movement."[37] But where did he locate these modern problems? Macpherson himself described his method as a "subjective use of inference."

Instead of the method of externalized observation, dealing with objects, I was going to take my film into the minds of the people in it, making it not so much a film of "mental processes" as to insist on a mental condition. I take the action, the observation, the deduction, the references into the labyrinth of the human mind, with its queer impulses and tricks, its unreliability, its stresses and obsessions, its half-formed deductions, its glibness, its occasional amnesia, its fantasy, suppressions and desires.[38]

Consequently, the director made an almost obsessive use of the close-up, in which light and shadow from taut skin and flickering muscle were used to evoke mood and meaning. As H.D. described a particular shot of Robeson, "We have here an exquisite pen and ink sketch of a negro head almost filling the space of the little frame allotted."[39] Post-static art, as H.D. characterized it, formally located modern problems in the psyche.

The effect of the modernist aesthetic in *Borderline* was to freeze

Robeson into a modernist ideal of the Negro male, outside of history. Macpherson insisted, however, that through his technique he was merely exposing the truth and essence of black masculinity. In reality, what he created was what haunted him: "a sense of *virility or solidarity of being* which was at once discernible as imperatively Negroid."[40] The subjectivity dissected and exposed by his camera work was in effect a product of his own modernist desires and anxieties surrounding the formation of masculinity in the modern world. Its racialization was a mediating device.

It was not that race was an issue that had to be overcome to allow for democratic or egalitarian masculine bonding to take place, but that race became the necessary ground upon which reflections about masculinity could take place. In this sense, a modernist racial consciousness was produced out of the dissecting gaze—rather than, as it was claimed, inherent in the subject itself. The Negro, as a creation of the modernist aesthetic, could never become a political comrade; and when Robeson himself determined to embody an alliance between art and activism for social change, his body was forever severed from the modernist aesthetic. What Muray, Macpherson, and, I will argue, Eugene O'Neill shared was a fascination with the dangerous potential for violence and anger *within* the black male body, at the expense of concern with the violence and anger *acted upon it*. It is in this sense that they also shared the dissecting gaze of the lynch mob.

For H.D., living in Europe, Robeson's black masculinity became a device for realizing her national identity. In a short story based on the Robesons' visit to Switzerland, entitled "Two Americans," Robeson became enshrined as a "seared bronze" character named Saul Howard. Howard's performance made Raymonde Ransome, the protagonist, a thinly disguised H.D., feel "that America was her home." H.D.'s racial fiction of Robeson speaks eloquently of her own desires and anxieties:

They met in a field of honor, herself entirely defeated, himself yet to be acclaimed for some kingship the world is not ready to recognize. He was no black Christ. He was an earlier, less complicated symbol. He was the Dionysus as Nietzsche so valiantly struggled to define him . . . his song flowed toward the world, effortless, full of benign power, without intellectual gap or cross purpose of hyper-critical consciousness to blight it. There was no swerving from the beginning, the root, the entire deep in-rooted power of his gigantic Being. He was really no person at all.[41]

This god-like symbol, powerful enough to apparently defeat or render passive the very protagonist/author who brings it into being, returns America to her.[42] In the guise of "gigantic" black male, Robeson trans-mits, like a syphon, the national body politic into her soul. While H.D. collaborated in a movie project to confront issues of inter-racial sexual-ity, her vision was clearly overwhelmed by her own racialized sexual desires, and yet these same sexual desires are fused with the desire for national belonging.

In 1925, the same year that Robeson posed for Muray, he starred in Oscar Micheaux's film, *Body and Soul*. The film is set in Tatesville, Georgia, a part of Du Bois's "black belt" in *The Souls of Black Folk*. In this film Paul Robeson plays a double role, a doubleness that introduces an interesting and very important sense of ambiguity into the modernist search for wholeness and strategies of inwardness. Micheaux confronted the fragmentation of modern life directly by splitting his protagonist into two men who, while identical in outward appearance, are complete opposites in personality and in moral and ethical intent, in other words, in their souls.[43] At the same time, neither the Reverend Isaiah T. Jenkins, alias "Jeremiah the Deliverer," an ex-convict, drunkard, and con-artist, nor his brother, shy and retiring Sylvester is what he appears to be. Rev. Jeremiah cultivates souls only to exploit them, while his double waits in the wings, appearing to be entirely without resources until the denouement.

The source for Micheaux's film *Body and Soul* is *Roseanne*, a play by Nan Bagby Stephens, a white woman from Atlanta, Georgia. Originally played in black face when it opened at the Greenwich Village Theatre in 1923, it was revived in 1924 with an all-black cast starring Rose

McClendon and Charles S. Gilpin. Gilpin, the *New York Times* declared, lacked authenticity, and soon after the play opened, Paul Robeson replaced Gilpin in the starring role of Cicero Brown.[44] Micheaux must have seen Robeson in the part and decided to turn the play, with its star, into *Body and Soul*.[45]

The plots of both play and film are very similar but not identical, and Micheaux also changes the names of his characters.[46] In *Body and Soul*, the main female character, Sister Martha Jean, is a modernist folk figure: a washerwoman who embodies the precepts of Booker T. Washington. (A rather stern portrait of him adorns the wall of her home, and the camera often places it in the center of the screen.) Martha Jean works hard—she is most frequently seen ironing—saves her money, and is the backbone of the local church. She worships her pastor, Jeremiah, who in her eyes can do no wrong, and she schemes to persuade her daughter, Isabella, to marry him. Isabella, however, wishes to marry humble Sylvester, Jeremiah's alter ego. Martha Jean refuses to let Isabella and Sylvester marry. Her blind devotion to Jeremiah and her determination that he shall be her son-in-law leads Martha to push her daughter into Jeremiah's clutches. Jeremiah rapes Isabella and forces her to give him her mother's life savings, which he needs to buy the silence of an old cellmate. The bribe is intended to save Jeremiah from being exposed as a fraud to his loyal flock, his only source of income. Jeremiah hounds Isabella out of town and is the direct cause of her death from starvation in a hovel in Atlanta.

The double persona that Robeson plays offers two choices to the black community. Its members can, individually, willingly consent to their own exploitation, or they can act collectively and turn to the unassuming people within their midst. This choice also presents two very different modes of masculinity: the one who flatters and cajoles and parades his manliness with epicurean delight, and the modest, shy, and retiring male who quietly waits in the wings of history. The black community of the film is shown to be responsible for encouraging the despicable Jeremiah: the owner of the local gambling den keeps him in liquor and regular "donations," for example, and when the community eventually decide to hound him out of town, Jeremiah accuses Sister Martha Jean of "pampering" him and thus being the cause of his moral and ethical degeneration.

Though Micheaux stays within the modernist problematic of body and soul, he tries to interrogate its frame. He explicitly rejects strategies of inwardness that would imply that one can interpret and produce meaning from the surface, or appearance, of the body. Indeed, he deliberately disrupts and challenges the individual production of social meaning. It is not until members of the community tell their individual stories to each other that they can reach a collective understanding of what their experiences mean. Micheaux's *Body and Soul* advocates, then, a collective response to the forces that threaten the well-being of a self-sustaining black community. The plot is finally revealed to be Martha Jean's bad dream. In the final scene she sits in a transformed home awaiting the return of Isabella and Sylvester from their honeymoon. Martha Jean has achieved respectable middle-class status, thanks to the success of Sylvester's invention; she has acquired a piano, and there are no more uplifting portraits of leaders hanging on her walls.

Perhaps the most intriguing link between Robeson and the body/soul problematic lies in a character that Robeson inspired but never actually played. In 1924, Walter White, assistant to James Weldon Johnson of the N.A.A.C.P., and supporter and promoter of young African American writers, wrote a novel entitled, *The Fire in the Flint*.[47] White hoped that a film would be made from the book, and he wanted Robeson to play the leading role. In addition to Robeson's obvious attractions, White evidently thought that Robeson projected other qualities that fitted his fictional protagonist, a doctor named Kenneth Harper. It is important to consider the cultural frames of reference surrounding Robeson that White was convinced could be drawn upon for the proposed film version of his novel.

Like Micheaux, White brought ambiguity to the body/soul dialectic but, unlike Micheaux, he engaged this dialectic in an exploration of the racial oppression of blacks by the dominant social order, and condemned white liberalism as being totally ineffective in challenging and countering the forces of oppression. White employed many of the cultural themes anchored in representations of Robeson, but he used them self-consciously to expose their limits as representations of black masculinity.

The physical characteristics of Kenneth Harper draw upon these conventions. He is described as having an athletic body, muscular and "well-proportioned" from "three years of baseball and football," which evoke Robeson's celebrated career as an All-American at Rutgers, and upon which many modernists, including Muray, drew in their representations of him.[48] But unlike Muray's liberal and, as I have demonstrated, compromised portraiture, White's ideal shares with Robeson himself a desire to incorporate intellect into the public performance of black masculinity. The fictional Kenneth's years at Atlanta University and medical school in the North had produced not just a professional but an educated and cultured individual, as White is at great pains to document. His hands are those "of a pianist, an artist, whether of brush or chisel or scalpel," hands as frequently full of literature as they are of medical instruments.[49]

As Micheaux did in his film, at the beginning of his novel White presents two distinct models of black masculinity to his readers: Kenneth Harper and his brother Bob. Kenneth may embody the Du Boisian precept of achieving black masculinity through becoming an intellectual, but he also believes in the doctrines espoused by Booker T. Washington.

> Booker Washington was right. And the others who were always howling about rights were wrong. Get a trade or profession. Get a home. Get some property. Get a bank account. Do something! Be somebody! And then, when enough Negroes had reached that stage, the ballot and all the other things now denied them would come. White folks then would see that the Negro was deserving of those rights and privileges and would freely, gladly give them to him without his asking.[50]

White describes Bob as "the natural rebel [for whom] revolt is part of his creed," whereas Kenneth "was the natural pacifist—he never bothered trouble until trouble bothered him."[51] Bob cannot understand why, with his skills, Kenneth would return from the North to Central City, Georgia, but Kenneth asserts that it is in the South, and only in the South, that he can both prosper and establish a clinic for black patients that could eventually gain a national reputation. Kenneth, in other words, believes that he can integrate himself and his work, by way of his community, into the modern national order. Bob, on the other hand, is convinced that their contemporary moment is worse for black people than before.[52]

The progress of the novel proves Kenneth wrong. Like Du Bois, White portrays political compromise and a dependence on the actions of "good white liberals" as a direct threat to a strong black masculinity. Though Kenneth becomes convinced by his brother that they have to work actively to undermine a racist social order, and Bob in his turn comes to believe in education and the power of the intellect, when they rebel, both are murdered by the white supremacists they oppose. White's novel uncannily predicts how quickly the liberal support of Robeson would disappear when he began to advocate not just the gradual transformation of a racist society but the need for its complete overthrow.

In Kenneth Harper, White creates a figure that represents the modernist desire "of what a Negro may be in the Golden Age"—a desire that was projected into so many public images of Robeson. Yet White exposes such desire as mythological. The liberal desire for a malleable black masculinity, a masculinity that could be shaped to satisfy white needs, is deconstructed in White's novel, and the ineffectiveness of white liberal sympathies is thus exposed and condemned. What we can see being invented in the work of Day, Muray, and Outerbridge, for example, is actively critiqued in *The Fire in the Flint*. While the title of the novel conjures up a vision of a power that lies under the surface and that waits to be released ("The fire in the flint never shows until it is struck"[53]), when violence and an active need to resist oppression are released in Kenneth and Bob, the southern sector of the society whose liberalism has so idealized this power, held in restraint in the modernist portraits of Paul Robeson, quickly responds by lynching them both. When Kenneth and Bob break out of the modernist mold of black masculinity and dare to gaze back at their oppressors, they are ripped limb from limb. The possibility that Kenneth's black masculinity can be incorporated into the national body politic is revealed to him as a vicious hoax, a political ploy that worked to pacify black men.

> "Superior race"! "Preservers of civilization"! "Superior," indeed! They call Africans inferior! They, with smirking hypocrisy, reviled the Turks! They went to war against the "Huns" because of Belgium! None of these had ever done a thing so bestial as these "preservers of civilization" in Georgia! Civilization! Hell! The damned hypocrites! The liars! The fiends! "White civilization"! Paugh! Black and Brown and yellow hands had built it! The white fed like carrion on the rotting flesh of the darker peoples! And called *their* toil their own! And burned those on whose bodies their vile civilization was built!
>
> Bob had been right! Bob had been a man! He'd fought and died like a man![54]

What makes Kenneth's and Bob's rebellion so dangerous to the prevailing order, and the reason why it has to be so viciously suppressed, is that it opposes modernist strategies of inwardness and the satisfaction of individual desire by advocating collective, not individual, rebellion against economic and political exploitation. Kenneth helps to organize sharecroppers into the National Negro Farmers Co-operative and Protective League. It is at the level of the representation of the possibility of collective black rebellion that the sort of modernist personas inhabited and performed by Robeson is most starkly contradictory.

Though White's novel was not produced as a film, Robeson was cast in a variety of roles of the rebellious or transgressive black male. But

these modernist roles actively worked to suppress the social and historical implications of collective resistance in order to contain black male
rebellion against social convention within the parameters of the psychological.

Eugene O'Neill's play, *All God's Chillun Got Wings*, which opened on
May 15, 1924, at the Provincetown Playhouse in New York City, is a
good example of this artistic containment. Starring Paul Robeson as Jim
Harris, *All God's Chillun* is an exploration of the social anxieties surrounding black male and white female sexual relationships and the
theme of miscegenation.[55] The play opens on a street corner in New
York where black and white neighborhoods intersect. As a dramatist,
O'Neill was very much a product as well as a producer of modernist
beliefs that black people felt and knew how to express emotions,
whereas white people could not. "People pass, black and white, the
Negroes frankly participants in the spirit of spring, the whites laughing
constrainedly, awkward in natural emotion. Their words are lost. One
hears only their laughter. It expresses the difference in race."[56] The
black soul, in other words, is offered as a resource to be tapped, a
well-spring of spirit.

As children, black and white play together. Ella Downey is a paradigm of white beauty, skin so white and lips so red that the other kids
nickname her "Painty Face," as if she were a doll. Jim worships her,
carries her books from school, and both fantasize about changing the
color of their skin: Ella wants to be black and Jim eats chalk three times
a day in an effort to become whiter. As they grow, black and white move
in increasingly separate worlds, and these childhood fantasies, a product
of a racist society, mutate and develop into obsessions that affect the
ability of each to mature into successful adults and influence the way
that Jim and Ella relate to each other. Jim, described as a "quiet-man-
nered Negro boy with a queerly-baffled, sensitive face,"[57] is studious
and diligent and has ambitions to become a lawyer. Yet, despite his
best intentions, he fails to graduate from high school the first time
and finds law school very difficult because he cannot perform in a white
society:

I swear I know more'n any member of my class. I ought to, I study harder. I work like the devil. It's all in my head—all fine and correct to a T. Then when I'm called on—I stand up—all the white faces looking at me—and I can feel their eyes—I hear my own voice sounding funny, trembling—and all of a sudden it's all gone in my head—there's nothing remembered—and I hear myself stuttering—and give up—sit down—They don't laugh. . . . They're kind. . . . They're considerate damn them! But I feel branded. . . .

And its the same thing in the written exams. For weeks before I study all night. . . . I learn it all, I see it, I understand it. Then they give me the paper in the exam room. I look it over, I know each answer—perfectly. On all sides are white men starting to write. They're so sure—even the ones that I know know nothing. But I know it all—but I can't remember any more—it fades—it goes— it's gone. There's a blank in my head—stupidity—I sit like a fool fighting to remember a little bit here, a little bit there—not enough to pass—not enough for anything—when I know it all.[58]

This failure to perform in school, a failure of the intellect, is in stark contrast to Jim's ability to act emotively. He tries to protect Ella from being sexually exploited by the local hero, Mickey, a prizefighter. Ella is resentful of Jim's interference in her life and refuses to speak to him for years. She becomes pregnant, is deserted by Mickey, and her child subsequently dies of diphtheria.

Ella and Jim meet again when both are failures and neurotic: Jim perpetually flunks his exams, and Ella is alone, friendless, and an outcast. Each thinks that the one can help the other to survive, and so they marry and move to Europe, but their psychological fantasies and obsessions have developed into psychoses. Their souls are torn by self-contradictory desires. Jim imagines that in France he can, at last, live as a man and prove his manhood to his wife, but at the same time he swears to be Ella's slave. As a couple they each contribute to the total psychological disintegration and disorientation of the other. Ella and Jim return to the United States, feeling that their relationship will improve if they have the courage to confront the consequences of their social transgression. Back at home, their situation worsens. Ella both wants and doesn't want Jim to pass his bar exam; she feels safer if he doesn't achieve his ambition to be a man. She vacillates between behaving like a harridan yelling racist epithets, and acting like a spoiled child demanding that Jim play the part of her slave.

O'Neill clearly intended the play to be an indictment of a racist social order, but in the staging of the processes of racialization the play turns deliberately away from exterior social and political effects and focuses instead on the way history affects interiority, the psyche. Both Jim and Ella are branded, psychologically damaged, and each plays a role in the destruction of the other. Like Muray, O'Neill utilizes modernist strategies of inwardness and is obviously fascinated by the deep power of emotion and anger kept restrained; he dissects the psyche of Jim as a black male in order to distill the essence of what has gone wrong, instead of dissecting the society in which his character lives. Yet the racist society's stamp marks those "branded" souls that disable the bodies from functioning. Nowhere is this clearer than in the mind and body split of Jim, whose intellect cannot function and who is reduced to endlessly recycling his historical role of slave, noble only in his utter devotion to his white rosebud doll of a wife. This unwillingness to confront contemporary social and political contradictions, a displacement of the social and political in favor of a focus on internal anxieties and desires, became a determining modernist aesthetic in the artistic production of the black male bodies that Robeson personified.

The cultural displacement of social ferment by emotional ferment is nowhere more evident than in O'Neill's play, *The Emperor Jones*, first performed in 1920 and starring Paul Robeson in 1924, and the 1933 film of the same title. The historical nightmare of the slaveholders of the antebellum South was fear of the rebellion of those they had enslaved, and the nightmare of the white-dominated racial state of the United States was the fear of black revolution and retribution, the possibilities of which had been all too clearly enshrined in the revolution led by Toussaint L'Ouverture that led to the founding of the world's first black republic. Haiti, as a black nation, took a central place in the North American modernist imagination when the United States began its occupation of that island with an invasion of Marines in 1915. Sidney Mintz has argued that "it was the United States occupation that gave the lie to Haitian sovereignty, and to the invincibility of its people."[59] The political and cultural meanings of the figure of Toussaint L'Ouverture and the specter of black rebellion were intimately connected to ideologies of black masculinity, and were highly contested among black and white intellectuals in the 1930s. Within the dominant cultural imagination, *The Emperor Jones* plays an important ideological role in the displacement of social and political anxieties of black rebellion, revolution, and revenge.

The frontispiece of O'Neill's play makes an indirect but pointed allusion to Haiti: "The action of the play takes place on an island in the West Indies as yet not self-determined by White Marines. The form of government is, for the time being, an Empire."[60] The condition of the Empire is, however, mere background. O'Neill focuses on the interiority of the black protagonist, Brutus Jones; his emotional ferment, rather than the social and political ferment, is the subject. Jones is "a tall, powerfully-built, full blooded negro of middle-age. His features are typically negroid, yet there is something decidedly distinctive about his face—an underlying strength of will, a hardy, self-reliant confidence in himself that inspires respect. His eyes are alive with a keen, cunning intelligence. In manner he is shrewd, suspicious, evasive."[61] Jones is not the exploited but the exploiter, an abuser of his power over the people he rules as Emperor.

The nature of the social conflict that produces a Brutus Jones, as O'Neill conceives it, is a struggle for survival: Jones learns how to live under the worst aspects of the capitalist system and is ultimately destroyed from within by his own "formless fears." The trajectory of the plot is a descent into Jones's unconscious, from which the audience learns of Jones's past history as a gambler and a murderer. (The film is less successful than the play as an intense exploration of an individual's psychic make-up, because instead of revealing his past through his psychological disintegration, it contains a rather crude prelude which dramatizes Jones's earlier life.)[62] As Jones plunges through the primeval tangle of his fears in an effort to escape from the residents of the island he has persecuted and abused, he is stripped of the trappings of his power and comes to question his own status as a civilized being. As the play progresses, it is evident that Jones's strong emotions are not under his control and that his past, which has made him what he is, cannot be repressed.

The cultural effect of the creation of Brutus Jones is a fundamental questioning of the possibility of rational black leadership. While O'Neill describes the oppression in Jones's past, and by implication recognizes it in black history, his play is an exploration of his doubts that that same history could produce rationality. The film examines the same doubts—history has produced a flawed character, the modern black man with a cancer eating away his soul. Thus the role of history in these performances is not to expose exploitation, an exploitation which continues into the present, but rather to provide an explanation for the irrationality of the present. In the final scene, Brutus Jones is reduced to being an abject slave, his voice and movements in rhythmic synchrony with the movements and voices of his persecutors as he is finally at one with his past. The Emperor tries to invent himself and dies a victim of his own mythology.

As a cultural text that became indelibly associated with Robeson, *The Emperor Jones*, like many of Robeson's film roles, situated within the black male subject of modernist imagining the social anxieties and tensions of modernity itself. Robeson recognized the pitfalls of these portrayals and, at times, defended his right as an actor to play any roles that he had the opportunity to play. In October of 1935 Robeson told a reporter for the *New York Amsterdam News*: "To expect the Negro artist to reject every role with which he is not ideologically in agreement. . .is to expect the Negro artist under our present scheme of things to give up his work entirely—unless, of course, he is to confine himself solely to the Left Theatre."[63] Robeson had been heavily criticized for some of his film roles, particularly in *Sanders of the River* (1935), which glorified

British imperialism, and for his role of Joe in *Showboat* (both the London theatrical production in 1928 and the film of 1937), which glorified "happy darkies." By May of 1937 Robeson was to state, unequivocally, that he was "sick and tired of caricatures" and saw no future in American films "because the South is Hollywood's box office." Indeed, during the thirties Robeson grew increasingly ambivalent about the roles he was being offered as he became aware of alternative possibilities open to him in Europe.

Following the filming of *Showboat* in Hollywood Robeson returned to England, in January 1936, to start rehearsing for C. L. R. James's play, *Black Majesty*, drawn from the work he was completing on Toussaint L'Ouverture, *The Black Jacobins*, published in 1938.[64] Robeson became fascinated with the Haitian revolution and the figures of Christophe, Dessalines, and Toussaint, and read avidly all the material on them that he could find.[65] James's portrayal of Toussaint as a complex combination of thinker and man of action, intellectual and revolutionary, was one that Robeson himself would increasingly adopt as his own.

In June of 1937 Robeson was calling for aid for the dependents of black Americans fighting in the Lincoln Brigades in Spain, because he felt that "The freedom of all the Peoples of the world is at stake," and that "there are literally hundreds of Negroes in the theatre and musical life who understand what a hunger for equality and love of mankind impelled me to take this step."[66] By November of 1937 Robeson had decided to become a part of the left theater movement, asserting that "When I step on to a stage in the future . . . I go on as a representative of the working class."[67]

Early in 1937 Robeson joined the General Council of the Unity Theatre, a collective that had developed out of the Workers Theatre Movement (WTM), sang at their fund raising events and celebrations, and became a tutor for its theater school.[68] He had developed a number of connections with some of its members. In 1934, in the Soviet Union, Robeson first met Herbert Marshall, who would produce *Plant in the Sun* for the Unity Theatre and direct Robeson in the film *The Proud*

Valley. Robeson had also worked with Andre van Gyseghem in 1935 in the play *Stevedore*, for which George Padmore helped recruit black cast members.[69]

As a member of the Unity Theatre, Robeson adopted their collective identity for *Plant in the Sun*; all actors were anonymous and any part could be played by any actor without notice.[70] As can be seen in the photograph of one of the scenes [Illustration XII], a different cultural aesthetic is at work. Robeson's body is neither a subject for individual psychological dissection nor the epitome of the internal emotional turmoil of black manhood. On the contrary, he is one among many, part of a social collective with shared aims and demands.

A prime example of this alternative aesthetic is the film *The Proud Valley*. What is so interesting about this particular film is that both Robeson's body and his voice are shown in new ways. In *Proud Valley* Robeson plays the part of an unemployed seaman who makes his way from Cardiff up the Rhondda Valley to look for work in the mines. He is initially integrated into the mining community through his voice. Walking through the streets of the small Welsh village, Robeson hears the village choir rehearsing for the Eistedfford. He adds his voice to theirs and is invited home to live with the family of the choirmaster, who gets Robeson a job in his team in the mines.

What follows is a story of collective loyalty, solidarity, and interdependence as Robeson helps the community through a crisis, exercises leadership, and, ultimately, sacrifices his life so that others will survive. The film shows images that are rare indeed. Medium shots that establish and emphasize Robeson's relationships with others, rather than close-ups that focus on his inner emotions, predominate in *Proud Valley*. Black manhood is integrated into the communal life of the white folk. The images of Robeson sitting at the dining table and around the hearth as an integral part of a white family are to be found nowhere else, and the scenes of his integration into the choir, blending his voice with theirs, offer a dramatic spectacle of the possibilities of interracial male bonding. And it is *male* bonding that *Proud Valley* is at pains to produce.

XII. Paul Robeson in the play "Plant in the Sun" (1937)
The Yale Collection of American Literature, Beinecke Rare Book and
Manuscript Library, Yale University

As the male breadwinner supporting the women at home, Robeson performs his masculine duty along with all the others, bonding specifically *as a man* with all the other men in the village.

Robeson completely rejected the division between art and politics in one of the most important speeches of his early career. To an audience gathered for a rally in the Royal Albert Hall in London in 1937, he declared:

> Every artist, every scientist, must decide NOW where he stands. . . .
>
> The artist must take sides. He must elect to fight for freedom or slavery. I have made my choice. I had no alternative. The history of the capitalist era is characterized by the degradation of my people: despoiled of their lands, their culture destroyed, they are in every country, save one, denied equal protection of the law, and deprived of their rightful place in the respect of their fellows.[71]

For the first time Robeson introduced the phrase that would reverberate throughout the rest of his life, eventually becoming the title of his autobiography, *Here I Stand*.[72]

In taking this stand Robeson assertively wrenched his body away from performative associations with modernist strategies of inwardness, and acted in defiance of all cultural aesthetics that denied or disguised their political implications. His heroic struggle in the cause of peace and freedom and his unwavering commitment to an internationalist politics of social transformation eventually placed Robeson uncompromisingly in opposition to the national discourse of race, nation, and manhood in the United States.

And you want me to sing
"We Shall Overcome"?
Do you daddy daddy
do you want me to coo
for your approval?
Do you want me
to squeeze my lips together
and suck you in?
Will I be a "brother" then?

ESSEX HEMPHILL

3

TUNING THE AMERICAN SOUL

We give at once the colorful, personal background of Negro "sinful songs" and the "life and works" of an artist who happened to be born with a black skin and with Negro barrel-house life, convict life and folk-lore for his artistic material.

John A. and Alan Lomax

One of Du Bois's major projects in *The Souls of Black Folk* was to locate black culture at the heart of the national community in the United States.[1] The spirituals, which Du Bois calls "sorrow songs," were central to this project. The final chapter of *The Souls of Black Folk*, "Of the Sorrow Songs," is devoted to a detailed discussion of spirituals *as folk songs* which are quintessentially American. This form of "Negro folk-song," Du Bois asserts, stands "not simply as the sole American music, but as the most beautiful expression of human experience born this side the seas. It has been neglected . . . half despised, and . . . persistently mistaken and misunderstood but it still remains as the singular spiritual heritage of the nation and the greatest gift of the Negro people" (p. 265). To Du Bois the spirituals bear the imprint of a history of struggle and oppression, embodying the historical articulation between race and nation; and they are important also because they harbor a faith in justice and hope for the future (p. 274). It is only in this last chapter

that Du Bois refers directly to the lyrics of the songs, although each
previous chapter is headed by measures of music that function as epigraphs. He does not reproduce any lyrics either in the epigraphs themselves or in the text which follows.[2]

Many critics have noted that it is impossible to establish genuine,
definitive versions of nineteenth-century African American folksongs.
Spirituals, like blues and their precursors, work songs and field hollers,
were constantly under revision by individuals and communities. Music
and lyrics were each subject to improvisation, making the tracing of
original sources of the composition or the identification of the composer a complex if not fruitless task.[3] Eric Sundquist has argued that the
words of the spirituals are missing from *The Souls of Black Folk* because,
"like any other complex set of allusions or quotations, they must be
known in advance or learned."[4] But in the final chapter Du Bois reflects
upon the relation between the ten "master" sorrow songs he includes
and the subjects of each of the chapters that comprise *The Souls of Black
Folk*, providing in this way his pattern of allusion between the songs and
his own words. I would argue that despite the absence of lyrics, the way
in which Du Bois uses his own essays functions as a *substitute* for these
missing lyrics. Indeed, I believe that the text of each chapter has a
specific performative role: each is a composition of improvised lyrics
upon the musical fragments that precede them. Du Bois does not reflect
directly upon the lyrics of the sorrow songs prior to his conclusion
precisely because he intends that his chapters be regarded as new lyrics,
new improvisations.

Sundquist's detailed reading of *The Souls of Black Folk* in his own
book, *To Wake the Nations: Race and the Making of American Literature*,
seeks to demonstrate how Du Bois set out to codify African American
culture and to provide proof of its existence.[5] In narrating the story of
the suffering of black peoples, the spirituals had to locate an "African
ground" and to tie "the prophetic dimension of the spirituals to an
African past,"[6] states Sundquist. But there is a profound problem with
viewing *The Souls of Black Folk* primarily as an ethnography which
codifies and offers proof of the existence of black culture. Such an

argument regards the text as being passive in its representation of black culture; it becomes merely a medium for its transmission. This view also ignores the important and very complex role of *The Souls of Black Folk* in the actual imaginative creation of a national, African American (as opposed to African) cultural presence, a presence which becomes a forceful participant in a cultural struggle over defining exactly what should constitute not just "black culture," but American culture.

The difference between the codification of black culture and active participation in its creation and meanings lies partly in whether we consider *The Souls of Black Folk* to be a performative text and partly in how we understand the representation of the national dimensions and significance of black culture. Sundquist argues that the inclusion of the sorrow songs, and Du Bois's "self-conscious identification with the preacher as a kind of cultural priest, fused . . . to the bardic function of epic and Romantic poetry . . . are the key elements that make the book the first properly theoretical document of African American culture."[7]

It is important to clarify the definition of Sundquist's "bardic function." The bard he associates with the communal singer, whose role was "antiphonal."

[H]is music answered or extended the preacher's text—a text that, in the predominant African American form, was already highly vocalized, largely improvised, and filled with the sonoral features that characterize much black (and some white) folk preaching—and thus exist in the liminal modality between word and music that defined the essence of spirituals as they shaded into shouts and sermons. Like the freely improvised spiritual, the black sermonic performance moves between song and chant. In its recourse to polyrhythmic structure and the inflections of blue tonality, the folk preacher's style moves in and out of the domain of the spiritual. . . . Metrical patterns and dramatic tension created out of the possibilities of sound itself shape the semantic content of the black sermonic style, and the audience participates through its own cries and shouts in the narrative creation of a lived scriptural story that has sources in the African chants of tribal law, historical narrative, and folk story.

But, Sundquist concludes, somewhat surprisingly, "there is no literal equivalent for such a folk performance in *The Souls of Black Folk*." "Whatever his experiments in genre and composition," Sundquist insists, "Du Bois for the most part hewed to a formal academic style of writing."[8]

If I have argued persuasively that *The Souls of Black Folk* is unquestionably structured through a pattern of call and response, then it should be clear that Du Bois does adopt and adapt the pattern of black sermonic performance. The call of his first chapter—"why did God make me an outcast and a stranger in mine own house?"—receives the response in chapters two through nine, which tell the story "of trouble and exile, of strife and hiding," a narrative that Du Bois considers characteristic of his ten master songs. In their turn, these eight chapters ask in various ways whether the strivings of black people for freedom are in vain: each chapter calls directly to the reader to consider whether to fight the struggles for emancipation, for the vote and for the right to exercise it, for access to equal education, and for an end to economic injustice. The final five chapters respond, assertively, that these struggles must continue to be fought.

Du Bois consistently uses forms of direct address and admonition to the reader, and provides, if not demands, the response. For example, in the opening chapter, "Of Our Spiritual Strivings," Du Bois employs the call: "Lo! we are diseased and dying . . . we cannot write, our voting is in vain; what need of education, since we must always cook and serve?" These words, in their rhythmic structure as well as in their intense pain, evoke the melodic structure and emotive themes of "Nobody knows the troubles I've seen," the strains that directly precede them. The call is continued and balanced by a response: "The bright ideals of the past,— physical freedom, political power, the training of brains and the training of hands. . . . Are they all wrong,—all false? No, not that. . . . The power of the ballot we need in sheer self defense,—else what shall save us from a second slavery. Freedom too, the long sought we still seek,— the freedom of life and limb, the freedom to work and think, the freedom to love and aspire" (pp. 51–52). The way in which these words improvise and draw upon the "music of an unhappy people" is complex. The text actually reproduces both the formal harmonic structures and the emotive content of the spirituals in a sermonic performance as effectively as his narrative history reproduces the story borne in the "lyrics of death and suffering and unvoiced longing toward a truer world" (p. 267). These are but a few examples of how *The Souls of Black Folk* does reproduce aspects of performance that directly evoke the cadences and tonalities of the sorrow songs, and that imaginatively enact and give voice and substance to the soul and spirit of the musical texts upon which Du Bois improvised.

However, it is also important to recognize that Du Bois actively creates and positions black culture as integral to the national culture in and through his text. The political struggles he recounts are struggles for citizenship and national belonging. This use of the spirituals, in *The Souls of Black Folk*, should be compared and related to the tours of the Fisk Jubilee Singers that obviously inspired Du Bois. As the Jubilee Singers brought the songs of oppression and of the desires and ambitions of an emancipated but still exploited people to a national and international audience, so Du Bois instills into the sorrow songs the symbolic power of a national melody which weaves black people into "the very warp and woof of this nation" (p. 275). It is in Du Bois's use of the sorrow songs and through his improvisations upon them that his political and cultural agenda is revealed. But the spirituals do not just set an agenda, they are the very means for imagining black people as integral to the national political community and for imagining black culture as a form of national culture.

Twenty-two years after Du Bois's book had been published, in April and May of 1925, Paul Robeson began his singing career with two performances at the Greenwich Village Theatre in New York.[9] Robeson's rendition of the spirituals brought him national recognition, and the timbre of his voice was considered capable of soothing America's

troubled soul. Robeson's biographer maintains that his debut performance, on April 19th, "propelled [Robeson's career] into a stratosphere
of acclaim."[10] A *New York Times* critic was ecstatic in his praise:

> Mr. Robeson is a singer of genuine power. The voice is ample for
> his needs, mellow and soft, but it is his intense earnestness which
> grips his hearers. His Negro spirituals have the ring of a revivalist,
> they hold in them a world of religious experience; it is this cry from
> the depths, this universal humanism that touches the heart . . . It
> was Mr. Robeson's gift to make them tell in every line, and that not
> by any outward stress, but by an overwhelming conviction. Sung by
> one man, they voiced the sorrows and hopes of a people.[11]

This enthusiastic description reveals a great deal about the reviewer's
own cultural meanings that he attributed to Robeson's performance.
Rather than speak to the history of exploitation and oppression embodied in the spirituals, the reviewer generalizes and essentializes, invoking
instead a "*world* of religious experience," and a "*universal* humanism."
What the reviewer admires is a purely emotive appeal of the power of
song to transport each individual soul above the mundane concerns of
everyday life and let it experience both the depths and the heights of a
universal spiritual feeling.

This type of response to Robeson assumed mythological proportions
in the United States in the 1920s. As Rose Henderson trumpeted in the
Southern Workman, "it is with the mellow, rhythmical songs of his race
that he achieves the most beautiful expressiveness and fervor. With
them he sways his hearers and fills the halls with a glamorous *elemental*
ecstasy which is unique and at the same time *universal*. In himself he
embodies the best qualities of his race—its vitality, its lovableness, its
beauty of voice and gesture, its emotional depth and glow."[12]

In both the *New York Times* review and in the *Southern Workman*
piece, Negroes, the people whose "sorrows and hopes" Robeson is said
to express and to embody, are the cultural vessels which contain liberal
amounts of spiritual and religious experience upon which the (well-

heeled) audience can draw. This particular imagining of Robeson is analogous to an imperialist desire which projects a terrain rich in resources, waiting to be exploited for the benefit of the nation-state. His performance of the spirituals was valued for bringing a forgotten "ecstasy" into the modern world, a world that had become afraid of its inability to experience intense emotion; he was a premodern conduit, capable of transporting America's soul to other worlds of experience by denying and repressing its brutal history.

Yet all attempts to present Robeson's performances of the spirituals as above the mundane experiences of everyday life must be situated within their historical moment, and their framework of modernist interpretation needs to be carefully analyzed. The first thing to note is the way in which Robeson's performance is frequently isolated from that of his accompanist, Lawrence Brown.[13] Although the concert performances of Brown and Robeson were not recorded, they signed a one-year contract with the Victor Talking Machine Company. Their first studio recording was made in July 1925, and we can still hear the results today.[14] Therefore it is possible to assess the significance of Brown's contribution to these performances.

Lawrence Brown was a musical arranger and collector of the spirituals, in addition to being a fine musician.[15] His association with Robeson needs to be understood as a musical partnership that has been called "one of the most superb musical collaborations in American musical history."[16] For the Victor recordings and for recordings made later in London for the Gramophone Company, Brown used a combination of his own arrangements and those of Harry T. Burleigh, who had published arrangements for the solo voice in 1916.[17] (Before Burleigh, the spirituals had been sung only in choral or ensemble arrangements.) Brown followed Burleigh in arranging spirituals for a solo voice accompanied by a piano.

The musical partnership of Brown and Robeson mounts a powerful challenge to interpretations of the spirituals which attempt to denude them of their historical, political, and cultural complexity. The power of their partnership lies in their harmonic articulation of the ways in which the spirituals lay claim to but also transform the religious tenets of the Judeo-Christian tradition. In replacing the multiplicity of harmonic possibilities in choral or ensemble performance by solo voice and piano, Brown's arrangements and Robeson's vocalization retain and reproduce the dialectical nature of this claim and transformation. The spirituals are heavily coded, giving voice to the experience of the oppressed while simultaneously condemning their oppressors through disguise and double-meanings. This complexity was frequently lost in interpretations of their performances.

Many critics contrasted the styles of Roland Hayes and Robeson. Carl Van Vechten regarded Hayes's spirituals as too "refined."[18] James Weldon Johnson felt that Hayes and Robeson reached their performative goals through opposite methods. Hayes, Johnson thought, employed "supreme artistry," while Robeson demonstrated "sheer simplicity, without any conscious attempt at artistic effort and . . . devoted adherence to the primitive traditions."[19] But this allegedly simpler and more authentic, or primitive, approach was, in fact, a very carefully crafted performance strategy by Brown and Robeson.

Though Van Vechten was one of the few critics who recognized the importance of Brown's partnership with Robeson, when he characterized their rendition of "Steal Away" as expressing "wistful resignation," he exposed the cultural and historical limits of modernist interpretations, his own included.[20] What Van Vechten heard as resignation is, in fact, disguised defiance. Robeson sings in a quiet and restrained voice, but the words "I ain't got long to stay here," which capture a slave's determination to escape captivity, are firmly underscored by Brown's chords. His arrangements are subtle but absolutely central to both the mood and tone of resolve. Brown plays underneath Robeson's voice, anticipating but also securing the chord changes.

In addition to form and interpretive style, Brown demonstrates a superb sense of timing as a musician and accompanist, frequently stretching harmonies to their limit. In "Hear the Little Lambs A-Cryin'," for example, Brown's chords are almost but not quite late, a technique he frequently uses to complement the wide range of Robeson's voice. The stretching of the musical interval allows for the incorporation of the full range of the double meanings. It is as if Brown opened up the space in which to "hear" and comprehend the multiple meanings of the words, so that words and tonalities melded in mutual triumph.

But modernist interpretations frequently played on the mere surface of the possibility opened up by Robeson's performance of the spirituals. This is true, for example, of the statue of Robeson sculpted by Antonio Salemmé and completed in 1926, which attempts to capture the pure spirituality of the singing [Illustration XIII].[21] Salemmé told Robeson to pose standing with his arms raised, hands lifted in supplication toward heaven, to think of "Deep River," and sing.[22] While the statue accentuates the act of religious supplication, an appeal directly to God, something crucial is lost in this representation, something that emerges from the musical relationship between Brown and Robeson. What this relationship brings to life is the need not only to reach the Promised Land in the afterlife but to improve the conditions of the present. When Robeson sang "Deep River," Brown's chords rose and fell with Robeson's glissando, forging both an appeal to God and a warning to those who oppress other men. Brown locates and anchors Robeson's slides securely in the present while reaching also toward the future. Salemmé's statue, on the other hand, seeks to sacrifice materiality for unearthly gain. The social contradictions between presenting the nude black male body as a vessel of pure spirituality and the actual social condition of black men in the United States occasionally became self-evident. When Salemmé sent the statue to Philadelphia, in 1930, in response to a request that it be exhibited, members of the executive committee of the city's Art Alliance "were filled with alarm at the prospect of a naked black man going on public display . . . because 'the colored problem seems to be unusually great in Philadelphia.'"[23] The statue was crated up and returned immediately.

To be an effective representative of metaphoric negroness, Robeson was stamped, by both black and white, with the signs of authenticity. Salemmé thought that what he had found in his model was "absolute

XIII. "Paul Robeson" (1926), statue by Antonio Salemmé
The Yale Collection of American Literature, Beinecke Rare Book and
Manuscript Library, Yale University

authenticity." Eslande Goode Robeson, to whom Robeson was married, believed that it was "some deep racial instinct" in her husband "that enabled him to identify more completely with the spirituals than could other black singers of the day." Avery Robinson, who transcribed the work song "Water Boy," declared that Robeson "was the only person who sang it exactly as the black chain gang" had been singing it when Robinson had first heard it.[24]

The first of Robeson's recordings was released late in 1925, and Langston Hughes hailed it as the means through which he, a northern black intellectual, could comprehend and identify with the black folk of the South: "The great truth and beauty of your art struck me as never before one night this summer down in Georgia when a little group of us played your records for hours there in the very atmosphere from which your songs came."[25] Authenticity, here, is attributed to a particular consciousness of the real. Robeson's recordings, made and purchased in the North, were taken into the South and used to authenticate the experience of Hughes and his colleagues vis-à-vis the southern black folk. This sort of cultural mediation between intellectuals and the folk facilitated a safer access to a *genuine* black experience for both black and white cultural producers.

From the beginning of his career, Robeson was presented as a black man who was not himself a bitter and angry product of an American history of injustice and persecution. A public acknowledgment of this *absence* of bitterness and hatred came to mark the way he was featured as a concert singer of the spirituals. This enabled the public to appreciate a cultural form that had its source in the history of slavery without the uncomfortable associations with exploitation and oppression that the nation would prefer to forget. "A satisfying thing about Paul Robeson is the completeness of his equipment for the thing he does. He is not only a magnificent physical figure with a splendid voice. His personality is a fascinating combination of warmth, simplicity, and understanding. He has superb poise and dignity, as well as humor and grace, passion and sensibility."[26]

Whereas Robeson himself, much like Du Bois, felt that the spirituals were cultural evidence of African American political struggles and consequently a weapon that could be used to great advantage, the white modernists who supported and promoted his concert performances used the artistic value of the spirituals to dissociate the songs from the brutal material conditions of oppression from which they came. As Robeson himself noted: "There is little audience in England and America for the things I feel like singing or playing. They want Negro religious songs from which they take, not the suffering, but the comfort of the resignation they express (not heeding that the song's cry for heaven is only a reflex from the Negro's having suffered hell on earth)."[27]

What the white public valued was the beauty and accessibility of Robeson's performance; the spirituals were turned into an aesthetic commodity for white consumption. Again, Salemmé's statue seems to personify this attitude. What was denied or held in abeyance was the central contradiction of the spirituals: their beauty and power gave expression to the politics of terror and brutality which produced them. Yet what Carl Van Vechten, among others, praised about Robeson's performance was the opposite of the cultural complexity I have described. When Van Vechten sponsored Robeson's first concert, he was convinced that the singer's appeal lay in his simplicity, not complexity.

I can never sufficiently record my admiration for the Negro Spirituals. The music of these simple, spontaneous outpourings from the heart of an oppressed race ranks with the best folk music anywhere and with a good deal of the second-best art music. The melodies have a strange, haunting appeal to which it is very difficult to remain indifferent. Indeed once they have become incorporated in the memory, they are there to stay. The words, too, crude though they often are, have the substance of true poetry.[28]

Van Vechten was such an important translator, transmitter, and producer of black cultural forms for white audiences that he could promote and advocate an art he dissociated from its complex roots while making a gesture toward the fact of oppression; this made it easy for the general public to do likewise without allowing the full expression of history to intrude.

That the complex history of terror, oppression, and exploitation could be held in reserve under the flag of aesthetic value relates closely to the images of Robeson's body in poses that suggest power held in reserve. Van Vechten described Robeson's performance in similar terms:

> There are times when [Robeson] reminds me, in the poignant simplicity of his art, of Chaliapin. It is typical of his acting that he never appears to be using his full prepotence. His postures and gestures and the volume of his voice are under such complete control and such studied discipline that he always suggests the possession of a great reserve force. . . . In singing, his voice retains its beautiful quality and the same sense of reserve power inherent in his acting manifests itself. His enunciation is impeccable—one never misses a word—and his interpretation is always clearly thought out and lucidly expressed.[29]

The formal qualities of control and discipline over voice and body gain political resonance precisely because Robeson is presented as a controlled and disciplined Negro: the consumption of his art could not threaten to disrupt the national constitution. The act of personal control and discipline was crucial to modernist interpreters of Robeson's performance of black manhood because, along with Van Vechten, they would rather understand the spirituals as being rooted in the "emotional ferment" of the Negro than be forced to recognize their source in the political and social conditions of exploitation.[30]

On November 5, 1939, Paul Robeson sang Earl Robinson's "Ballad for Americans" on the CBS radio program, *Pursuit of Happiness*. The performance received national acclaim, and Robeson was asked to rebroadcast it on New Year's Day.[31] The song was recorded in 1940 and was featured in Robeson's highly successful singing tour of that year.[32]

In "Ballad for Americans" the conventional cantata expands the framework of its classical form, with a multiplicity of voices in chorus, dialogue, and monologue. This complex mixture of forms, it could be said, musically transforms the dominant narrative history of race and nation into a narrative of ethnicity and class. One cultural critic has argued that Robeson's version of "Ballad for Americans" was "the anthem" of the "Popular Front public culture," which, "Under the sign of the 'people' . . . sought to forge ethnic and racial alliances, mediating between Anglo American culture, the culture of ethnic workers, and African American culture, in part by reclaiming the figure of 'America' itself, imagining an Americanism that would provide a usable past for ethnic workers, who were thought of as foreigners, in terms of a series of ethnic slurs."[33] Robeson's performance of "Ballad for Americans" offers a significantly different understanding of race, nation, and manhood from that of the spirituals. It is also a good example of how a performative moment can, at once, incorporate an earlier genealogy, discursively dislodge it, and create an alternative narrative while drawing upon the familiarity of the audience with the racialized aesthetics derived from Robeson's body.[34]

The song recounts the formation of the United States as a history of the struggles of ordinary people. As a part of a left-wing cultural movement, Robeson's version of "Ballad for Americans" relates to his commitment to working with radical theater groups in the United Kingdom and his film role in *Proud Valley*. In the United States Robeson was a figure who could hold together the contradictory racial narratives of the nation but, at the same time, the song itself threatened to disrupt those conventional narratives.

It is quite a remarkable performance. The narrative of "Ballad for Americans" tells a history of conflict—an alternative narrative to "patriotic spouting." Starting with the Revolutionary War of 1776, the nation is born out of "thunder" and "storm." The adoption of a constitution that guaranteed equality to all is juxtaposed with the inequalities involved in the actual building of the nation ("some liked to loaf while others dug ditches"); and the musical line is interrupted by the haunting strains of "Let My People Go." The rule "of the people, by the people, and for the people" is contrasted with "the everybody who's nobody . . . the nobody who's everybody."

As the narrator, Robeson is situated at the crux of these conflicts and contradictions, and at the climax of the cantata his voice claims a series of identities named by the occupations of working people: "engineer, musician, street cleaner, carpenter . . . the et ceteras. . . . And the and so forths that do the work"; by race or ethnicity, "Irish, Negro, Jewish, Italian"; and by religious affiliation, "Baptist, Methodist, Congregationalist, Lutheran." "Ballad for Americans" does not attempt to resolve the history of conflict it narrates; on the contrary, it concludes that the struggle to found an equitable nation continues: "Out of the cheating, out of the shouting, out of the murders and lynching. . . . Our marching song will come again." Such fusion of radical politics with a popular poetics enabled Robeson to combine his political commitments with his public performances for a brief period of time, until the House Un-American Activities Committee issued a citation against him, which led not only to the loss of his civil rights but also to an attempt by the state to muzzle him. The tenuous links that held ideologies of race, nation, and manhood in a fragile alliance through public representations of Robeson's black male body were violently broken once he decided to take a stand for causes which could no longer be accommodated or tolerated by dominant ideals of Americanness.

The contradictions embedded in any attempt to incorporate black culture into the national culture can be clearly seen in the relation of patronage between John Lomax and Huddie Ledbetter, better known as Leadbelly. In 1933, John Lomax became a consultant to the Library of Congress and, accompanied by his eighteen-year-old son Alan, began a tour of the southern states in order to collect and preserve American folksongs, using an electric recording machine. Determined to rectify the paucity of black folksongs in the national collections, the Lomaxes were the first to collect African American folk music out in the field.[35] Hoping to record songs that had not made it into mainstream American music and to locate musicians who had been isolated from the influence of white culture, John and Alan Lomax traveled to areas of the South where black people constituted a high percentage of the population.

The Lomaxes were in rebellion against what Zora Neale Hurston derided as "the spirituals dressed up in tuxedos": black culture dressed up for national consumption in the pretentious garb of European high cultural forms. Rather than disguising or denying the folk roots of black music, the Lomaxes sought to present to the American public the results of their wanderings: an authentic black folk figure performing authentic black music. However, what exactly constituted this authenticity was determined and defined by the Lomaxes themselves.

John Lomax regarded the type of concert performance made so popular by Paul Robeson as inauthentic. Robeson singing "Go Down Moses," for example, was regarded by folk purists as evidence of a cultural compromise.[36] When he sang the words "oppressed so hard, they could not stand," or

> No more shall they in bondage toil
> Let my people go
> Let them come out with Egypt spoils
> Let my people go,

he eradicated the vocal slurs and slides which anthropologists of folk culture consider characteristic of African American music. The complexities of polyrhythms were replaced by a simple chord structure synchronized with a crisp and unambiguous diction. But, I would argue, although some of the formal techniques associated with African American musical performance had been altered, what Robeson created was a performance which was unapologetic and uncompromising in its claims to vocal power and human dignity. In other words, what the Lomaxes objected to was Robeson's respectability. In many ways, Robeson on the concert stage represented Du Bois's ideal embodiment of black manhood. His performances projected a racialized cultural aesthetics that insisted on its right to be considered central to the constitution of the national cultural community. The Lomaxes had in mind a very different embodiment of black manhood, one that would occupy a significantly different relation to the national community than that of Robeson.

The political project of the Lomaxes was to cast the black male body into the shape of an outlaw. John Lomax intended to recover an unadulterated form of black folk music, and in the process actually invented a particular version of black authenticity. The Lomaxes worked not only with many unquestioned assumptions about what constituted black cultural authenticity, but they also hoped to locate black people in what they imagined to be their natural environment. John Lomax characterized the relation between cultural form and the site of its production as analogous to that between an animal and its habitat: "[Black] folk singers render their music more naturally in the easy sociability of their homes and churches and schools, in their fields and woodyards, just as birds sing more effectively in their native trees and country."[37] Because of his particular interest in the work songs of gang laborers, John and his son traveled to work camps that employed black labor almost exclusively, and they spent a good deal of their time visiting prisons and penitentiaries. In view of his romantic analogy of the birds in the trees, one can only ask whether John Lomax regarded prisons and penitentiaries not only as sites which were isolated from the influence of white culture, a dubious and somewhat ironic assumption, but as part of the native habitat of black people.

John and Alan Lomax met Huddie Ledbetter in the summer of 1933 in the Angola Penitentiary, Louisiana, while he was serving a six- to ten-year sentence for assault with intent to murder, and they returned a year later to make further recordings. The legend is that Leadbelly sang his way to freedom: a recording of "Goodnight, Irene," delivered to Governor Allen by John Lomax, persuaded Allen to commute Leadbelly's sentence. Six years earlier, Leadbelly had supposedly sung for Governor Neff of Texas and obtained a pardon from serving a forty-year sentence for murder in the Texas state prison system. The fact is that Leadbelly's release from Angola was a purely routine matter under a "double good time" law,[38] but the legend became one element in the invention of a complex persona that negotiated the contradictions between Huddie Ledbetter, the black male ex-convict, and Leadbelly, the national embodiment of folk culture.

John Lomax's construction of the figure of Leadbelly was complex and contradictory. He drew upon his basic premise that black people were to be regarded as a part of nature, as opposed to civilization, and described Leadbelly in language that suggested the elemental, as if the singer were a force of nature, like a volcano, which could appear benign on the surface while it held an unlimited potential for power and destruction underneath.[39] Here, for example, is one reminiscence: "'I'm thinkin' in my heart,' once Lead Belly said when we asked him why, when he was about to sing, he sat so quiet. That was his way before an audience—to sit silent and relaxed, this man of terrible energy, turning over in his mind God alone knows what thoughts, then, at the signal, to let loose his hands and his voice."[40] This particular concept of black manhood was developed into an aesthetics of black folk culture for the national media when the Lomaxes took Leadbelly on tour. Such an aesthetics is particularly significant, not only because it reveals Lomax's own desires and fears, but because these desires and fears are then reproduced as commercially marketable qualities, as desires and fears that the public will be eager to consume.

For a feature-length article in the *New York Herald Tribune* headlined "Sweet Singer of the Swamplands Here to Do a Few Tunes Between Homicides," John Lomax explained to the journalist and his readers that Leadbelly was a "'natural,' who had no idea of money, law or ethics and who was possessed of virtually no self-restraint."[41] This particular description "sells" Leadbelly to the public as an elemental force threatening to disrupt all that could be considered to be markers of a civilized community—as, simultaneously, that which was most desired and that which was most to be feared. Thus the tremendous power that Huddie Ledbetter exercised over his twelve-string guitar, a power which could totally mesmerize an audience, was compelling precisely because it was the power of a man who was strong enough to kill.

Lomax's version of his own personal relationship with Leadbelly negotiates the terrain of pleasure and danger that exist in bourgeois imaginings of the black folk and invents a particular understanding of the nature of the historical conflict between white and black men in North America. As Lomax tells it, this is a story of learning how to live with a constant threat; it consists of a series of daily efforts on Lomax's part, and by implication on the part of all middle-class white men, to stay in control of this unpredictable destructive force. Through their patronage, the Lomaxes created in the person of Leadbelly an icon of the uneasy relation between race and nation that enshrined him as a national folk singer but, simultaneously, confirmed his status as an outlaw against whom constant vigilance is required.

The Lomax account of how Leadbelly came to be employed by them caught the national popular imagination. According to John Lomax, on September 16, 1934, Leadbelly came to his hotel in Marshall, Texas, seeking work. Lomax replied to this demand by asking Leadbelly if he was carrying a gun. The conversation ensued as follows:

"No, suh, boss, but I'se got a knife."

"Let me see it."

He handed me the knife, which I opened and balanced on my hand. It had a long, narrow blade, sharpened to a razor edge.

"Lead Belly," I said, "down in Austin I have a home and a lovely lady for my wife; also a very dear daughter, Bess Brown. I hope to live a long while for their sakes. If you sometime—when we are driving along a lonely road—decide that you are going to take my money and car, you need not stick this knife into me. Just tell me and I'll hand you my money, get out of the car, and let you drive on."

"Boss," he said, as if deeply moved, "Boss, dis is de way I feels about you: Ef you got in a fight wid a man an he start to shoot you, I'd jump in between an' ketch de bullet myself an' not let it tech you. Boss, please suh, lemme go wid you; I'll keep your car clean an' drive jes' like you tell me. I'll wait on you day an' night. An' boss, you'll never have to tie yo' shoes again ef you'll lemme do it."[42]

So Lomax employs a man whom he acknowledges to be a danger to his person as a personal servant and driver and pays him one dollar a day. At the same time, John and Alan Lomax become the patrons of a singer for whom they created an image and a national reputation. A contract Leadbelly signed with them both stipulated that he receive only one third of all his earnings, after all expenses had been deducted, and that John and Alan Lomax split the remaining two thirds. Inventing a figure of the black folk could be a profitable enterprise!

This story of Leadbelly as an ex-convict, a walking time-bomb who becomes a faithful retainer, and of the Lomax "discovery" and patronage of the folk singer of the age, became encoded as the Leadbelly legend, and the man himself was made to personify black manhood in a *March of Time* newsreel, filmed in February 1935.[43] *March of Time* newsreels were a combination of filmed events and studio enactments of events.[44] This particular newsreel opens with the title, "Angola, LA!" followed by a scene of actors posing as black convicts, in uniforms with broad stripes, gathered into a circle at the feet of John Lomax and Leadbelly, the latter playing his guitar and singing "Goodnight, Irene." Leadbelly is standing center-screen, and Lomax sits beside his recording equipment. The voiceover announces, "To Louisiana State Penitentiary goes John A. Lomax, Library of Congress curator, collector of American folksongs." The voiceover thus immediately establishes Lomax's credentials and national authority and interprets for the audience the meaning of a scene in which an obviously unarmed white man is surrounded by black convicts with not a guard in sight.

It is instantly obvious who is in control of the situation. Lomax is the first to speak: he issues the command "Just once more, Leadbelly," and adjusts the dials on the recording machine. Leadbelly repeats the chorus, and this dialogue follows:

"That's fine Leadbelly, you're a fine songster. I have never heard so many good nigra songs."

"Thank you sir, boss. I sure hope you send Governor Allen a record of that song I made up about him 'cos I believe he'll turn me loose."

"Leadbelly, I don't know this Governor. You mustn't expect too much of me."

"Well, Governor Neff from Texas, he turned me loose when he heard the song I made up about him."

"So, you were in a Texas penitentiary too, Leadbelly?"

"Yes sir, I got thirty-five years for murder but it wasn't my fault, a man was trying to cut my head off."

"Leadbelly, I'll try."

"Thank you sir, boss, thank you." [He strikes chords on his guitar.][45]

The scene then changes to a hotel room in which John Lomax is busy typing. The inter-title explains the passage of time and the scene: "Three months later the travels of curator Lomax take him to Marshall, Texas." Cutting to the lobby we see Leadbelly, dressed in overalls with a bandanna around his neck, interrogating the hotel reception clerk in order to locate Lomax. We have to assume that Lomax was successful in negotiating a release for Leadbelly and thus are prepared for Lomax's subsequent role as Leadbelly's patron. Upon being told the floor and room number, Leadbelly rushes up the stairs leaving the clerk shouting ineffectually, "Hey, hold on a minute!" Cutting to Lomax's room, Leadbelly knocks and is told to enter.

"Boss, here I is."

"Leadbelly, what are you doing here?"

"No use trying to run me away boss, I came here to be your man. I got to work for you the rest of my life. You got me out of that Louisiana Pen."

"You can't work for me, you're a mean boy. You killed two men."
"Please don't talk that way boss."
"Have you got a pistol?"

In this scene Leadbelly's second imprisonment, for assault, is transformed into murder to make the potential threat to Lomax's life even more plausible. However, Leadbelly states that he does not have a gun and hands over his only weapon, a knife; that dialogue has been cited above. Then the scene concludes:

"You'll never have to tie your shoestrings any more as long as you keep me with you."
"Alright, Leadbelly, I'll try you."
"Thank you sir, boss, thank you. I'll drive you all over the United States and I'll sing songs for you. You'll be my boss and I'll be your man."

The *March of Time* newsreel brought the Lomax legend of Leadbelly into popular culture, but it also did more than that. Through this particular performance, the creative reconstruction of the relationship between Lomax and Leadbelly imaginatively resolves some social and cultural anxieties of masculinity: anxieties about whether white men can effectively control black male bodies, and anxieties arising from the struggle of white men to control their own fear of black male bodies.

Leadbelly, who actually liked to present himself to the public in a suit and bow tie, is seen in the newsreel clothed in a costume of overalls and bandanna created by the Lomaxes as an authentic folk image for his public performances. This aesthetics of the folk invents a fictive ethnicity of blackness which, when performed, enabled Leadbelly's incorporation into the national community. Pete Seeger has described Leadbelly as "soft-voiced" and "meticulously dressed"; Moses Asch remembers his "aristocratic appearance and demeanor"; but it is the Lomax-invented black folk persona of Leadbelly as a mean and dangerous "nigger" who has be tamed by his white male patron that is elaborated into the cultural fiction which, in turn, legitimates and authenticates his music.[46]

In the newsreel, Leadbelly's celebration as a national folk figure is actually dependent upon the confirmation of his status as a dangerous outlaw. Although in the final scene Leadbelly's music enters the Library of Congress, to be housed "with the Declaration of Independence," says the voiceover, it is significant that Leadbelly himself is not present on this occasion. Instead, it is John Lomax and a group of Library of Congress officials, all respectably dressed in sober suits and ties, who control the terms of entry of Leadbelly's recordings into the National Archive.

John and Alan Lomax produced the music of Leadbelly as a form of national music, in the same sense as W. E. B. Du Bois had claimed, in *The Souls of Black Folk*, that the spirituals were a national form of culture. But Du Bois and the Lomaxes invented very different genealogies of race, nation, and manhood to back up their contentions. Each genealogical narrative had very different consequences for the imagined political configuration of a racialized democratic national community, but both evoked the possibility of integration and eventual harmony in their own distinct terms; neither imagined that a state of equilibrium between the nation and racialized men could be accomplished only through revolutionary means, the complete destruction of the racist society which gave the concepts of race, nation, and manhood historical meaning. It is to the imagining of black manhood as not only potentially dangerous but as a revolutionary force that I now turn.

When my brother fell
I picked up his weapons
and never once questioned
whether I could carry
the weight and the grief,
the responsibility he shouldered.
I never questioned
whether I could aim
or be as precise as he.

ESSEX HEMPHILL

4

BODY LINES AND COLOR LINES

In the 1930s a number of male intellectuals, both black and white, created historical discourses of black manhood in the service of a revolutionary politics which argued for the violent overthrow of all racialized social formations. The figure of Toussaint L'Ouverture emerged in this period as a popular model for creating contemporary images of a revolutionary black male consciousness. The revolution in Haiti, frequently linked to rebellions by those enslaved in North America, was used as the historical landscape in which the possibilities for black male autonomy, self-government, and patriarchal black nationhood could be enacted.[1] The work of C. L. R. James is particularly important in this context. This chapter will trace the varied and discrete stages through which James developed representations of autonomous, self-determining, revolutionary black manhood, and analyze the gendered aesthetics of body lines which are inherent in its imagining.

During the 1920s and 1930s intellectuals of the left in general, and black American and colonial intellectuals in particular, became increasingly concerned about their intellectual, political, and moral responsibility to voice the need for radical social change.[2] Those intellectuals who were also cultural producers envisioned this dilemma as an issue of representation—how to represent the "people," the "folk," or the "masses" and how to imagine the relation between the intellectual and the people, or the leader and the masses.

C. L. R. James's first attempt to tackle this issue was through the figure of a white male in a book entitled *The Life of Captain Cipriani*, published in 1932.[3] The narrative structure he employed, which he called "political biography," is further utilized and developed in two of his other important works of the thirties, a novel called *Minty Alley* (1936), and *The Black Jacobins: Toussaint L'Ouverture and the San Domingo Revolution* (1938).[4] James was convinced that the form of political biography was "the best means of bringing before all who may be interested the political situation in the West Indies today." The narrative form of *Captain Cipriani* prefigures the narrative structure of *The Black Jacobins*: each of the class formations is introduced into the text as if it were an individual on the stage of history, a character through whom history must be understood and whose actions are both determined by and determine the social conditions in which he or she lives.[5]

James chose Cipriani for the individual subject of his collective political history because, "During the last eighteen years, he has been engaged in a series of struggles against the bad manners, the injustice, the tyranny, and the treachery of Crown Colony Government."[6] This was James's first attempt to articulate an anticolonial politics. Though not by any means a revolutionary text of the sort he would write later, *Captain Cipriani* begins an argument that would eventually integrate anticolonialism and revolutionary politics.

> . . . in the colonies any man who speaks for his country, any man who dares to question the authority of those who rule over him, any man who tries to do for his own people what Englishmen are so proud that other Englishmen have done for theirs, immediately becomes in the eyes of the colonial Englishman a dangerous person, a wild revolutionary, a man with no respect for law and order, a person actuated by the lowest motives, a reptile to be crushed at the first opportunity. What is at home the greatest virtue becomes in the colonies the greatest crime.[7]

James's position is that although opposition to a colonial regime is interpreted by the colonialists as being a revolutionary and dangerous act, in fact anticolonialism in the West Indies should be regarded as the logical outcome of dominant English ideologies of humanitarianism and "fair-play." The outlaw was being outlawed by the very ideologies instilled into him as a colonial subject. The very inclusion of "bad manners" in James's list of items against which the colonized had to struggle reveals the extent to which James defined himself, and other West Indian intellectuals, in relation to ideologies of Englishness, under the influence of which they themselves also lived. But he was also acutely aware of how and why the colonized were regarded as dangerous by those who had to control them—the analogous process was at work in the Lomaxes' construction of the black folk figure of Leadbelly. The subject people represented a danger which, by the very possibility of its imagining, justified the imposition of draconian controls over the potentially rebellious masses.

Captain Cipriani, described as Trinidadian male hero and nationalist, is as much a historical product of the colonization of the West Indies by Great Britain as he is a force in opposition to it. In one of his speeches he declares: "Today we have our Trinidad, to which we are all so proud to belong. The proudest boast of the Englishman is that his home is his castle, and if I can be satisfied that I can imbue the same spirit into the souls of our children, boys and girls, who will be the men and women of to-morrow, to make your West Indian homes your castles, then I feel that a great and good work will have been well and truly done."[8] Captain Cipriani is represented as not only harboring dreams of equality with Englishmen, but exemplifying them in his own actions. James recounts how his hero proved himself a superior man among men with the British West India Regiment in Europe during World War I, in which he was a fierce defender of the regiment against the injustices suffered at the hands of the commanders of the British Army.

As a model for future black male heroes, Cipriani is important because he represented the interests of the people. Although Cipriani, a planter, was not *of* the people, James describes him as a man who put aside the interests of his own class: "He has a cocoa estate, but . . . his political work caused him to neglect it so much that had not two of his supporters taken it over he would have lost it long ago. . . . He represents the people so well, chiefly because he is so much one of them."[9] This image of a political leader deliberately acting against the interests of his own class would become very significant in James's later reflections about the influences of class and race upon the potential of black men to assume positions of leadership.

In an aside, *Captain Cipriani* actually links for the first time two of the author's major concerns, politics and cricket. For while the subject of the book is a Trinidadian politician and West Indian colonial politics, the book is dedicated to Learie Constantine, the great cricketer, "For reasons not private but public, and quite unconnected with cricket."[10] In *Captain Cipriani* as well as in his cricket journalism, James sought to develop a theory of a direct, unmediated relation between the heroic male figure and the people, a theory which used a cultural aesthetics of body lines in direct opposition to the modernist strategies of cultural producers like Muray or Macpherson, who regarded themselves as necessary mediators and interpreters of art.

Nowhere is James's ideal of the black male hero as one inspiring as well as expressing the social passions of the people clearer than in his writings on cricket. To him the male body on the cricket field was a work of art—not an art that needed to be interpreted or translated by an intellectual, but an aesthetic experience of the body that could be grasped immediately and directly by the spectators themselves.[11] For example, of George Headley, James wrote: "He is a Negro, finely built but short and small, and only a careful judge of physique would notice him in a crowd. But at the wicket no one can miss his mastery. He is of that type which uses a bat as if it is an extension of the arm. Ease, poise and balance, he has them all. Good as his footwork is for defensive play, it is even better in the way he makes ground to the ball."[12] If no (male) spectator could fail to recognize the beauty of this movement as art, none need feel excluded from identifying with the bodies of male cricketers, for this beauty, James insisted, was not the exclusive preserve of the young male.

Barnes not only is fifty-nine, but looks it. Some cricketers at fifty-nine look and move like men in their thirties. Not so Barnes. You can almost hear the old bones creaking. He is tall and thin, well over six feet, with strong features. It is a rather remarkable face in its way, and could belong to a great lawyer or statesman without incongruity. He holds his head well back, with a rather long chin lifted. He looks like a man who has seen as much of the world as he wants to see. . . .

When every man was placed to the nearest centimetre Barnes walked back and set the old machinery in motion. As he forced himself to the crease you could see every year of the fifty-nine; but the arm swung over gallantly, high and straight.[13]

Just as in *The Black Jacobins* James paid homage to Toussaint L'Ouverture when he was an aging revolutionary hero, "a man who has seen as much of the world as he wants to see," so he portrayed S. F. Barnes as the bowler whose aging male body still demanded recognition and respect for its lines of beauty and power in action.

As Sylvia Wynter has eloquently stated, in James's writing the aesthetic "is no less material than the *economic*." And she continues:

The expropriation of the means of aesthetic perception, of the mechanics of critical judgement are no less and perhaps far more terrible with respect to its consequences than the expropriation of the means of production. The means of providing for material existence are vital, but so too are the means of enacting, exercising, developing the innate faculty—*the eye for line and for significant form*, an eye physical in earlier circumstances where the natural environment was the dominant challenge, now conceptual and aesthetic in a situation where man's greatest obstacle to the realization of his powers, to the free play and development of his faculties, is now the socio-cultural environment.[14]

I would add to Wynter's insight that James's aesthetic is precisely what is central to his revision of the treatment of the black subject within modernity.

James could narrate the story of West Indian politics in the form of the individual political biography of Captain Cipriani because his principal character had transcended his class interests and placed his skills at the service of the people. In a similar fashion, James could use the story of cricket for revealing the social passions and desires of the people because, although the game had been introduced into Trinidad by the colonizers, it was subsequently claimed and transformed by the colonized. In this process the history embedded in the cultural form changed. Once a sport of British artisans, cricket later became a cultural form of the English bourgeoisie; in Trinidad, however, cricket carried the history of the country's racial and class formation.

> Trinidad, for instance, has had a curious history, and English, French, Spaniards, Chinese, Portuguese, Negroes and East Indians are represented there. All except the Portuguese play. There was a Chinese team fifty years ago. There is one today. The East Indians have many teams. Besides which various nationalities play together in the same teams. The little village of fifty houses may not have a church. It may lack a schoolhouse, but the cricket pitch is there. . . .
>
> During the long peace which followed Waterloo, the British officers in the West Indies relieved the tedium of those remote spots by playing cricket, and it is certain that in that hot climate the "natives," that is to say, the Negroes, did most of the practice bowling and fielding. Fifty years ago in Trinidad a relation of mine, a blacksmith, a tremendous hitter and wicket-keeper, played with a team composed of the doctor, the warden, the magistrate and the other white notabilities of the district, ten white men and a Negro. His mother had been a slave on an estate still owned by some of the brothers who played in the team.[15]

Written in 1933, for the British journal *The Cricketer*, this sketch precedes by 30 years the astute cultural analysis of cricket as "the clash of race, caste and class," an analysis that critics argue is not present in his work until *Beyond a Boundary*, published in 1963.[16] Yet it is important to locate this analysis and its cultural aesthetics in James's writings of the thirties in order to understand the complex ways in which his narrative strategies were linked to each other, in gendered ways, across the various kinds of texts he authored in the 1930s.

In praise of James on the occasion of his eightieth birthday, E. P. Thompson declared:

> What an extraordinary man he is! It is not a question of whether one agrees with everything he has said or done: but everything has had the mark of originality, of his own flexible, sensitive and deeply cultured intelligence. That intelligence has always been matched by a warm and outgoing personality. He has always conveyed, not a rigid doctrine, but a delight and curiosity in all the manifestations of life. I'm afraid that American theorists will not understand this, but the clue to everything lies in his proper appreciation of the game of cricket.[17]

I would add that we certainly cannot understand the centrality of concepts of masculinity to the development of James's radical politics unless we appreciate the ways in which his readings of Marx, Lenin, and Trotsky were grafted onto his conception of the history of cricket as a political biography of colonial manhood.

Thus, although it is not until *Beyond a Boundary* that James reflects upon the two major political and social influences in his life, literature and cricket, the two recurring tropes through which he tracks the emergence of his political consciousness, the same elements already constitute a political *unconscious* in his 1930s accounts of cricket as a culture of colonial masculinity. Just as W. E. B. Du Bois believed it was essential to state that he himself, as a man, embodied the history of the people whose story he recounts —"need I add that I who speak here am bone of the bone and flesh of the flesh of them that live within the veil?"[18]—so James presents his own biography as being at one with the people of the West Indies through the reference to his ancestor, the blacksmith, only one generation removed from being enslaved.

Without a doubt, it was through cricket that James confronted the racialized colonial politics of Trinidadian society. He perceived the history and practice of cricket as the arena where the politics of colonization, of class and race rivalries, were contested.[19] As James described it in *Beyond a Boundary*, "the various . . . clubs represented the different social strata in the island within clearly defined bounds," the "social passions" of the players and the crowd used "cricket as a medium of expression," and thus "the cricket field was a stage on which selected individuals played representative roles which were charged with social significance."[20] While James claims that he "was in the toils of greater forces than [he] knew," that "[c]ricket had plunged [him] into politics long before [he] was aware of it," he also admits that "When [he] did turn to politics [he] did not have too much to learn."[21] Upon reflection, James feels he made a fairly seamless transition from being a cricketer and cricket journalist to being a radical political activist in support of the movement for West Indian self-government and autonomy, and in favor of using revolutionary means to throw off the yoke of imperialism. The transition was seamless precisely because ideologies of masculinity, whether conscious or unconscious, were already shaping his understanding of the performative politics of cricket *and* his idea of how colonialism should be opposed.

On one occasion in 1933, when James was not explaining the history of West Indian cricket to a British readership but writing for a West Indian readership, he assessed the chances of the West Indian team defeating the English in contentious language that called for subordinating all other interests in the cause of defeating the English. In reference to the extremely controversial debate about body-line bowling, James describes the English batsmen as "childishly helpless against the fast bowling" of the West Indies.

> Whether Grant [the captain] will allow himself to be frightened by these English critics is an important question. If he breaks the morale of his fast bowlers by expressing doubts as to whether the tactics of Constantine and Martindale are fair, the West Indies should flay him alive. The English had no mercy on the Austra-

lians. Now that the tour is over and the Ashes won, nearly every English writer and cricketer with the most bare-face effrontery condemns body-line bowling, but when the Australians protested they shrieked to high heaven that there was nothing in it and the Australians were merely squealing. This is our chance and if weakness and lack of a sense of realism in the high command makes us lose it, then our blood be upon our own head. . . .

For let every good West Indian know that, after watching cricket here [in England] and carefully weighing my words, I have no hesitation in saying that in cricket, as in many other things, West Indians are among the most highly gifted people one can find anywhere. The English have money, thirty times our population, vast organization, every conceivable advantage. Yet with all that, we could hold our own. Our trouble is that we have not yet learned to subordinate everything to winning. Under modern conditions to win you have got to make up your mind to win. The day West Indians White, Brown and Black learn to be West Indians, to see nothing in front to right or left but West Indian success and the means to it, that day they will be grown up. Along with that it will be necessary to cultivate any number of fine speeches, noble sentiments and unimpeachable principles. But these you must indulge in before the struggle, *cricket or whatever it may be*, and also long after the struggle is over.[22]

I quote this passage at length because here, in James's cricket journalism, is the nub of the dilemma Toussaint L'Ouverture faces in *The Black Jacobins*. In this passage, the cricket pitch becomes the battleground out of which nationhood must be forged. Toussaint would face the overwhelming might and arrogance of France, and his crucial role as a leader was to convince the people to sacrifice everything to claim their independence. Here also James anticipated his later reflections upon the nature of revolutionary leadership: he believed it was extremely important to realize that the leader has as much the ability to undermine the cause of the people and thus sabotage the revolution as to inspire the masses to victory. We can also see in this passage a provisional draft of James's view of the relation between history and human agency: namely, that the nature of the existing conditions determines the requisite action. His reference to the "modern conditions" of colonialism, which require a specific response, prefigures his account of the San Domingo revolution, in which he concludes that men make their own history only within the conditions given to them by history.[23] Upon the cricket pitch the struggle is between those who wish to retain and those who seek to overthrow the hierarchical relationship between colonizer and colonized.

Yet we should recall that James claimed two major political and social influences in his life, and it remains for me to explore the role of literature in the Jamesian construction of black manhood—the sort that colonialism tried hard to deny or suppress.[24] James's education as a scholarship boy in Trinidad forced him to recognize the contradictions an intellectual experienced in the colonies. His assiduous study and practice of the art of fiction and criticism led him to draw two conclusions about his life. As a colonial intellectual, he felt alienated: "Intellectually I lived abroad, chiefly in England. What ultimately vitiated all this was that it involved me with the people around me only in the most abstract way." At the same time, he recognized his deep commitment to literature as an instrument of social reform.[25]

When James left for England in 1932, he had already embarked upon a number of projects that combined his interests in literature and cricket. While working as a schoolteacher, James had contributed columns on cricket to local newspapers and had started to work with Learie Constantine on his biography. Constantine financed James's trip to England so that the biography could be completed, and when it was finished, he used his influence to secure James a position as cricket correspondent for the *Manchester Guardian*. Two manuscripts accompanied James on his journey to England, the political biography of Captain Cipriani and the novel which would later be published as *Minty Alley*.

At this moment in his life James was determined to become a novelist.[26] Before leaving for England, he had contributed short pieces of fiction to two Trinidadian journals, the *Trinidad* and the *Beacon*.[27] As I described more fully elsewhere, contemporary debates about proletarian literature and arguments about the revolutionary role of intellectuals influenced the circle of Trinidadian intellectuals to which James belonged.[28] In his fiction James attempts to explore their alienation, which was also his own.

In his short stories and in *Minty Alley*, James wrote about a particular sector of the Trinidadian working class and the culture of the barrack yards. His fiction, however, is extremely self-conscious of the vicarious nature of its authorial point of view. While his writings on cricket effortlessly reveal the political nature of the direct and unmediated relation between cricketers and spectators and their shared social passions, his fiction is hampered by the awkwardness of the literary devices used to place the working-class characters and their social and political passions in relation to the narrator's or protagonist's point of view. In *Minty Alley*, for example, the protagonist, Haynes, watches the lives of the barrack-yard occupants through a hole in the wall of his room.[29] This problem of the writing itself clearly reproduces contradictions of class; in addition, there is the problem of negotiating, within a fictional landscape, the difficulties of establishing a political alliance between intellectuals and the masses. What also demands our attention are the startling contradictions of the politics of gender, not only within the culture of the barrack yard, but between its residents' and the authorial or protagonist's point of view, and between James's writing on cricket and his fictional worlds.

Grant Farred has a very interesting explanation of the significance of a crisis in James's life which, he argues, revealed the political contradictions embedded in James's social and political existence as a cricketer, and in his social and political existence as an intellectual and literary figure.[30] Farred argues that it "is not unusual that a single ideological crisis should constitute the most formative political event in an intellectual's life. [But] It is certainly rare . . . that such a moment should arrange itself around the choice of a sporting institution."[31] As James himself recounts in *Beyond a Boundary*, becoming a member of a cricket club in Trinidad was fraught with considerations of "race, caste and class." When James had to choose what club to join, making this decision "plunged [him] into a social and moral crisis which had a profound effect on [his] whole future life." As James describes the situation, each club "represented the different social strata in the island within clearly defined bounds."[32] Highest in prestige were the Queen's Park Club, whose members were mainly white and wealthy, and Shamrock, which catered to the old Catholic families and was exclusively white. Clearly, neither was open to him. The remaining three were Stingo, whose members James described as "plebeians," Shannon, "the club of the lower-middle class," and Maple, whose members belonged to the brown-skinned middle class to whom "Class did not matter so much . . . as color."[33]

James considered that Stingo lacked sufficient status for him to join it and therefore limited his choice to Shannon or Maple. As Farred argues, insightfully, "Stingo . . . was a cricketing institution James could admire but with which he could never affiliate himself. It was fixed in a class location beyond James's most radical political imaginary; Shannon represented the limits of that imaginary."[34] That James could choose between Shannon and Maple, even though he was dark, was because he was not only a talented cricketer but had a reputation as "a man cultivated in literature."[35] According to Farred, "James' position in his society was unprecedented since the 'coming' cricketer was also a 'coming' intellectual."[36]

James's choice of club is especially significant in illuminating the formal aspects of his fiction. His decision to join Maple placed him in exactly the same relation of distance to the Shannon cricketers that we observe exists between the narrator's or protagonist's point of view and that of the inhabitants of the barrack yards in his short stories and novel. James states that he "became one of those dark men whose 'surest sign of . . . having arrived is the fact that he keeps company with people lighter in complexion than himself.' " This decision, though it reinforced his position in his social and intellectual milieu, "cost me a great deal. For one thing it prevented me from ever becoming really intimate with W. St. Hill, and kept Learie Constantine and myself apart for a long time. Faced with the fundamental divisions in the island, I had gone to the right and, by cutting myself off from the popular side, delayed my political development for years."[37] And yet, although becoming a "Maple man" had been, in retrospect, an impediment to establishing close relationships with the men he most admired, at the time James wrote about those same men *as if* they all shared the same social and political passions. I would argue that the intimacy James sought is imaginatively projected into his essays on cricket, which in fact formally *assume* a shared social and political point of view. Such an assumption may have been an invention, but it served a political purpose in its imagining of a national political consciousness.

This formative social and ideological crisis of James's intellectual life has been generally regarded as a crisis of "race, caste and class." But I would argue that the political and social relations of gender overdetermine the other crisis. Indeed, that particular historical moment in James's life and the contemporary moment in which cultural critics write about James share many implicit assumptions about masculinity, including the gendered segregation of sporting institutions.

Like the masculine world of the cricket pitch and cricket club, the barrack yards is a gendered landscape, but the world of the working class is imagined overwhelmingly through figures of women. There is an interesting analogy between the Stingo cricket club, which lacked sufficient class status to attract James, and the use of women to indicate the lack of status of the world of the alley. The class divisions of James's fictional world are gendered: the masses are feminized; the point of view of the intellectual/middle-class protagonist is masculine. When James abandoned fiction to write about revolutionary politics and revolutionary heroes, he also gave up trying to write about women.

The gendering of James's fiction takes a number of interesting forms. In *Minty Alley*, for example, the bridge that enables Haynes to cross into the world of the working class and stop being a mere vicarious observer of their life is an act of sexual conquest. Sexual intimacy between the young female character, Maisie, and Haynes is the means by which Haynes comes to "know" the intimate details of the life of the yard; sexual familiarity with the female body and familiarity with the body of the proletariat are representationally collapsed and fused. As Haynes concludes, "To read of these things in books was one thing, to hear and see them was another."[38] Simultaneously, this moment also acts as a marker of Haynes's sexual maturity: becoming a man and gaining the knowledge he needs to represent the masses are likewise combined. Haynes "realized that whatever he said would carry weight with them, and with this realization came a sense of responsibility and increasing confidence."[39] From this point on, Haynes plays an essential rather than peripheral role in the lives of the occupants of the barrack yard: women become actively dependent upon him and increasingly subservient in servicing his domestic and sexual needs.

The social passions of the barrack yard parallel the social passions of the cricket pitch, but the complexities of the roles of intellectual, political activist, and revolutionary hero play themselves out only in the actions of male heroes or those who represent the masculinized class formations. In James's fiction, men who allow themselves to be subjected to the will of women rather than dominate them are granted no fictional agency in the events of the plot, and, in *Minty Alley*, they even die.[40]

In contrast to his fiction, James's essays on cricket describe a representational landscape that can embody the world of colonial politics because that world is all male. The cricket pitch was where and how the colonial relations of class and color were fought, a field in which men struggled against men, defending wickets, hurling fast balls, body to body and bowlers to batters, in a confrontation that rendered invisible the politics of gender which shaped the practices and ideologies of the sporting institution. Intellectual practice, racial politics, and cricket were, and continue to be, unquestioningly imagined within a discourse of autonomous, patriarchal masculinity.

The effect of the multiple ways in which gender overdetermines James's representation of the clash of "race, caste and class" is that he reduces the material deprivations and the marginality of everyday existence of the people in the barrack yards to the materiality of the female body. If the relations of working class people consist of relations among and between women, then the representation of the life of the poor is brought down to the level of gossip, petty jealousies, and female rivalries: a bitter series of confrontations that cannot transcend the social condition which produce them. Indeed, instead of embodying the hopes and desires for a liberated future, the residents of the barrack yard in *Minty Alley* disappear from the landscape altogether in its closing pages. In stark contrast, on James's cricket pitch the national conscience and the consciousness of nationalism, the soul, the political spirit of the nation, are not only discursively masculinized but transcend the individual bodies of the men in the struggle of a greater social and political collectivity to assert itself as historical agent.

Clearly, in the general political and social imagination the birth of future generations is most frequently feminized, while revolution is often represented as a homosocial act of reproduction: a social and political upheaval in which men confront each other to give birth to a new nation, a struggle frequently conceived of in terms of sex and sexuality. This is not a social convention that applies only to the work of James; it is common to most male writers of the period. So, for example, a young girl asks Gabriel Prosser in Arna Bontemps's novel, *Black Thunder*: "Anybody what's studying about freedom is apt to catch his death, one way or another, aint he?" To which Prosser replies, "But it's men-folks job just the same. It ain't a fitten way for women's to die."[41]

In *Black Thunder*, the energy that a male revolutionary hero needs for an act of rebellion is the same he uses in the sexual act; it comes from a reservoir easily depleted by women, who therefore threaten to be a potential drain on the power of manhood. When he asks old Catfish Primus to work some magic to aid their revolt, Gabriel warns him: "Mind out what you's doing there, Old Primus. Don't get yo' conjur mixed up hear. . . . I just don't want no hand to make the women's love me when I needs to be fighting. That's all."[42] Bontemps also makes direct comparisons of rebellion with sex and women: "always big-talking about what booming bed-men you is. Always tryin to turn the gals' heads like that. Well, let's see what you is good for sure 'nough. Let's see if you knows how to go free; let's see if you knows how to die." Many phallic images reinforce this duality: "Juba sat astride Araby's bare back, her fragmentary skirt curled about her waist, her naked thighs flashing above the riding boots . . . the warm body of the colt straining between her clinched knees"; Criddle "knew the feel of warm blood . . . [who] knew, as well, that his scythe-sword was ready to drink. He could feel the thing getting stiffer and stiffer in his hand."[43] The phallus continues to be an important signifier of revolutionary black manhood in contemporary fiction. In Samuel Delany's *Nevèryon* series of novels, the rebel leader, known as "The Liberator," is named "Gorgik," and the word "gorgi," we learn, means penis.[44]

In Guy Endore's novel *Babouk*, based on the Haitian rebellion, the protagonist gives birth to the revolution in another way: he breathes life into captives through his story-telling as they lie in their own filth, close to death, in the belly of a slave ship. Babouk's stories also enable the enslaved on the Galifet plantation to maintain their humanity, to recognize the injustices they suffer and to imagine freedom. In this manner, the principal character becomes not only a rebel leader but the actual conduit through which the seeds of rebellion are planted in the minds and hearts of his followers.[45]

James's portrayal of the conditions which give rise to revolution shows most clearly how he conceives the way men make history. James takes a statement from Karl Marx's *The Eighteenth Brumaire of Louis Bonaparte* to structure *The Black Jacobins*: "Men make their own history, but they do not make it just as they please; they do not make it under circumstances chosen by themselves, but under circumstances directly encountered, given and transmitted from the past."[46] This requirement—that we understand the actions of all people in the context of and as shaped by the particular circumstances of their history—is transformed by James into a sexual union between men and history, a union which produces, sustains, and nurtures the life of the revolution. Of Toussaint, James states:

In him, born a slave and the leader of slaves, the concrete realisa-
tion of liberty, equality and fraternity was the *womb* of ideas and the
springs of power, which overflowed their narrow environment and
embraced the whole of the world. But for the revolution, this
extraordinary man and his band of gifted associates would have
lived their lives as slaves, serving the commonplace creatures who
owned them, standing barefooted and in rags to watch inflated
little governors and mediocre officials from Europe pass by, as
many a talented African stands in Africa to-day.[47]

James believes that Toussaint and, by implication, all successful revolutionary leaders need this combination of maternal and paternal reproductive capacity. He sees Toussaint not only as a fearless warrior and
stern but loving father to his people, but as a man with the ability to
bear and realize the revolution; James grants to the black male hero the
organs of female reproduction. If it were not for the revolution, Toussaint and his associates would have lived their lives in the feminized role
of domestic servitude, as did the women of the barrack yards in *Minty
Alley*. But while the heroic male figure can appropriate the reproductive
power of the female body to bring forth an act of rebellion, feminization
alone can only mark the abject.

In many complex ways the politics and language of gender overdetermine the representation of the black male rebel and produce a politics
and aesthetics of the black male body. It is in this sense that the racialized and gendered discourse of the body in these subversive and revolutionary texts connects with the politics of the black male body enacted
in the practice of lynching. As an erotic and phallic form of masculinity
was assumed and subsumed in representations of the black male rebel,
so the eroticism and phallic nature of the ritual dismemberment of black
male bodies was an essential part of the attempt to deny to black men
the power to resist, rebel, or revolt.

James's two versions of *The Black Jacobins*, the play and the political
biography, were inspired by the intellectual ferment generated by a
group of black radicals involved in anticolonial and anti-imperialist poli-

tics in Britain in the 1930s.[48] Written at a time when, as he eloquently describes, "in the stillness of a seaside suburb . . . could be heard most clearly and insistently the booming of Franco's heavy artillery, [and] the rattle of Stalin's firing squads," *The Black Jacobins* speaks directly to the politics of antifascism and the possibilities of resisting and overthrowing colonial rule: "From no classes of people have Negroes suffered more than from the capitalists of Britain and America. They have been the most pertinacious preachers of race prejudice in the world."[49] In the context of antifascism, anti-imperialism, and antiracism, James's work is an explicit critique of the aesthetics and politics of modernism.[50] As Sylvia Wynter has said, for James "The aesthetics is the politics."[51]

The Black Jacobins rejects, absolutely, the liberal politics of compromise and seeks to rewrite the history of the role of black men in the formation of the modern world. In the process of reconstituting modernity, James also produces an alternative model of intellectual practice, a different methodology for the writing of history. "The writing of history becomes ever more difficult," he says in the introduction, particularly in relation to finding the balance between art and science, the role of man in the shaping of historical circumstance and the role of circumstance in shaping the acts of man. If, traditionally, "historians have been more artist than scientist," writing their well-crafted narratives of man bringing into being and destroying societies "because they saw so little," then in his own age the reverse had become true: "great men [are portrayed as] being merely or nearly instruments in the hands of economic destiny." James concluded that neither emphasis produced historical accuracy and asserted instead that the historian had to be a dialectical thinker. "Great Men make history but only such history as it is possible for them to make. Their freedom of achievement is limited by the necessities of their environment. To portray the limits of those necessities and the realization, complete or partial, of all possibilities, that is the true business of the historian."

This is particularly true for accounts of revolutions. James felt that they were the sort of volcanic eruptions in which it was all too easy for historians to become consumed by "caprice and romanticism," to be captivated by the chaotic surface debris thrown into view rather than concentrate on excavating for the roots of the upheaval. To avoid such whimsicality and nostalgia, James sought "not only to analyse, but to demonstrate in their movement, the economic forces of the age; their moulding of society and politics, of men in the mass and individual men; the powerful reaction of these on their environment at one of those rare moments when society is at boiling point and therefore fluid." In *The Black Jacobins* he concludes, "The analysis is the science and the demonstration the art which is history."[52]

In writing this revolutionary history, James is challenging the patronizing attitude of liberals who think that freedom in the modern world was granted to black peoples through liberal philanthropic endeavors,[53] and countering simplistic opposing views which would claim that freedom was merely grasped with two hands and stolen.[54] What is at stake in *The Black Jacobins* as a thesis of history? As an intellectual, James seeks to be a practitioner of his theory of history as he simultaneously molds his revolutionary hero, the outlaw, in the form of his thesis of history. Like Guy Endore's Babouk, James not only recounts the history of the emancipation; he presents the recognition of the necessity for self-emancipation as a precondition for the emergence of the revolutionary leader. Yet the seeds of a vision of emancipation are planted in the narrative by the intellectual as historian.

In Toussaint, James enacts his dialectical thesis of history. His hero has elements of education; he is an organic intellectual.[55] As Toussaint reads the revolutionary doctrine of Abbé Raynal, he becomes aware of the need for a revolutionary leader: "A courageous chief only is wanted. Where is he, that great man whom Nature owes to her vexed, oppressed and tormented children? Where is he? He will appear, doubt it not; he will come forth and raise the sacred standard of liberty."[56] However, just before Toussaint makes this comment, James makes it clear that the enslaved do not need "education or encouragement to cherish a dream of freedom." As they sang, "We swear to destroy the whites and all that they possess; let us die rather than fail to keep this vow."[57] The narrative tells the story of the people "feeling its way to revolution"[58] and thus emerging as a historical agent, enlisting the reader in imagining the possibility and the necessity for such agency. In this manner, *The Black Jacobins* both argues for and brings into being revolutionary subjects.

Toussaint laid the foundations of a lasting black state and "made the history that he made because he was the man that he was." Yet it is James who, with his astute political and cultural analysis of body lines and color lines, enables his readers to imagine the possibility of the existence of a revolutionary black manhood that, both individually and collectively, gives birth to an independent black nation state.

Wizards. All of them. Wizards.
Gravel in their throats.
Worrying the line
Horn to bleeding lips.
Fingers thrashing white keys
cascading black.

ESSEX HEMPHILL

5

PLAYIN' THE
CHANGES

Beyond my campaign to free Nevèrÿon's slaves, whom will I ally myself with next? Will I take up the cause of the workers who toil for
wages only a step above slavery? Or will I take up the marginal work-
less wretches who, without wages at all, live a step below? Shall I ally
myself with those women who find themselves caught up, laboring
without wages, for the male population. . . . For they are, all of them—
these free men and women—caught in a freedom that, despite the
name it bears, makes movement through society impossible, that
makes the quality of life miserable, that allows no chance and little
choice in any aspect of the human not written by the presence or
elision of the sign for production.

    I do not know . . . not because desire clouds my judgment, but be-
cause I had the misfortune once to *be* a slave.

               Samuel R. Delany, Neveryóna

        Feeling free, after all, is the whole act of jazz.

              Miles Davis

Two contemporary autobiographies are absolutely central to any consideration of black manhood: *The Motion of Light in Water: Sex and
Science Fiction Writing in the East Village 1960–1965*, by Samuel R. Delany (1988), and *Miles: The Autobiography of Miles Davis* (1989).[1] Al-

though written in the 1980s, they offer incisive and informative reflections upon the formation of black male subjectivities in the 1950s and 1960s in the United States.

If the work of C. L. R. James focuses on revolutionary claims to black male autonomy and self-determination, the works of Samuel Delany and Miles Davis can be regarded as detailed explorations of the nature of that freedom which revolutionary activity uses as its rallying cry. Though neither autobiography directly addresses the political actions of the Civil Rights Movement of the time, each narrative, like the written and musical texts Delany and Davis, respectively, produce, interrogates the limits and possibilities of freedom in urban America.[2] Neither writer takes the sense of "freedom" for granted; on the contrary, each searches for its meaning, moving beyond the problem of *freedom from* and exploring the nature of freedom itself. However, I will argue that while Delany's vision of freedom extends outward to include women and all working people, Davis's concept of freedom remains limited to the misogynistic world of jazz, and it manifests itself principally in the musical relations among the male instrumentalists with whom he worked. While concentrating on Miles Davis, I will be in constant dialogue with the memoirs, fiction, and essays of Samuel Delany, using the latter as, at times, a harmonic and at other times a dissonant, counterpoint to and extended riff upon the concepts of masculinity in Davis's work.

Davis and Delany's explorations of the nature of freedom take place in urban environments, most often New York City. In their respective autobiographies each artist creates and then immerses himself in a particular vision of the city in order to produce the definitions which will shape his masculinity. New York City, as locus of cultural power, also authorizes and anchors the creative inspiration of each artist.

Miles and *Motion of Light in Water* open on the eve of manhood: Davis and Delany are both eighteen when they experience events of great significance to the type of men they will become. In 1944, Davis hears a performance of the music that will shape his life, an experience of such passionate intensity that he compares it to sex:

Listen. The greatest feeling I ever had in my life—with my clothes
on—was when I first heard Diz and Bird together in St. Louis,
Missouri, back in 1944. I was eighteen years old and had just
graduated from Lincoln High School. . . .

When I heard Diz and Bird in B's band, I said, "What? What is
this!?" Man, that shit was so terrible it was scary. I mean, Dizzy
Gillespie, Charlie "Yardbird" Parker, Buddy Anderson, Gene Am-
mons, Lucky Thompson, and Art Blakey all together in one band
and not to mention B: Billy Eckstine himself. It was a
motherfucker, Man, that shit was all up in my body. Music all up in
my body, and that's what I wanted to hear. The way that band was
playing music—that was *all* I wanted to hear. It was something.
And me up there playing with them.[3]

The moment of recognition by the boy who was leaving boyhood and
the man who was about to be, is registered directly by and throughout
the body as the feeling of desire. Hearing Eckstine's band leads Davis
directly to New York, undertaking a journey not only to follow these
musicians and their music, but to make himself into a man in their
image.

Motion of Light in Water also opens with an experience that pro-
foundly shaped Delany's future: "For most of my life, if it came up, I
would tell you: 'My father died of lung cancer in 1958 when I was
seventeen.' "[4] Delany has to come to terms with this loss in order to
define the meaning of his own manhood and to determine his future
career as a writer.[5] The evening of his father's death, Delany ignores the
protests of his mother and goes out into the streets of New York: "I
went walking by Riverside Park. Dead leaves mortared the pavement
around Grant's Tomb. For some reason, sitting on one of the benches
beside the public mausoleum, I took my shoes and socks off to amble
barefoot on the chill concrete, beneath the mercury-vapor lights, note-
book under my arm. I'd been trying to write an elegy."[6] Delany's direct,
bodily contact with the city beneath his feet is as physical an experience
as that of Davis. It is also formative of the creative and sexual desires of

the man who will emerge from this moment. These streets will not only provide the landscape for Delany's fiction but are also the paths he will wander in search of homosexual encounters. Issues of artistic creativity are interwoven so tightly with the threads of sexual longing in both autobiographies that it is impossible, at times, to unravel them. However, the recounting of the death of the father also poses a particular problem for Delany as writer.

In 1978, a scholar preparing a bibliography of Delany's work sent a letter pointing out that, as Delany was born in 1942, he could not possibly have been seventeen in 1958. Delany's carefully considered response to the anomaly he created is unexpected but challenging:

> [B]ear in mind two sentences:
> "My father died of lung cancer in 1958 when I was seventeen."
> "My father died of lung cancer in 1960 when I was eighteen."
> The first is incorrect, the second correct.
>
> I am as concerned with truth as anyone—otherwise I would not be going so far as to split such hairs. In no way do I feel the incorrect sentence is privileged over the correct one. Yet, even with what I know now, a decade after the letter from Pennsylvania, the wrong sentence still *feels* to me righter than the right one.
>
> Now a biography or a memoir that contained only the first sentence would *be* incorrect. But one that omitted it . . . would be incomplete.[7]

Thus it is not only the fact of his father's death that is of great significance to his emergence as a man and as a creative artist; the point is also that his own representation of that death epitomizes the ambiguity and complexity of the creative process itself, a process in which history and memory often conflict and contradict one another.

For the Davis of *Miles* the issue of freedom relates to two clearly gendered spheres of existence. He seeks freedom *from* a confinement associated with women, and freedom *to* escape to a world defined by the creativity of men. One of the conventions of jazz performance is the echoing or restatement of themes from other jazz instrumentalists. Jazz autobiographies frequently reproduce this musical convention, establishing the male ancestors of their authors with the rigor of the "begat" recitations of patriarchal lineages in the Old Testament.[8] In *Miles* Dizzy Gillespie and Charlie Parker are Davis's "father figures," and he recalls how he tried to imitate Freddie Webster, his "main man" during his early days in New York.[9] But the influence of these musicians is not limited to the conventional role of the instrumental mentor. From the opening pages of his autobiography Davis consciously seeks to replace the influence of women with the influence of men in his life: "I still remember when I was just a kid, still wet behind the ears, hanging out with all these great musicians, my idols even until this day. Sucking in everything."[10] "I wanted to come to New York in the first place, to get in to the jazz music scene that was happening around Minton's Playhouse in Harlem, and what was going down on 52nd Street, which everybody in music called 'the Street.' That's what I was really in New York for, to suck up all I could from those scenes. Julliard was only a smokescreen, a stop over, a pretense I used to put me close to being around Bird and Diz."[11] The jazz "street" of New York City is the place of Davis's rebirth, as a man and as a musician. What that picture projects, however, is the ambiguity of men reproducing men without women. Davis's male instrumentalists provide the nourishment which will sustain him and enable him to grow, but do they stand for metaphoric breasts providing essential nutrients and immunities, or is the evocation homoerotic, and what is suckled is the creative inspiration drawn from the phallus? I suggest that both meanings exist in uneasy juxtaposition.[12] For Davis's male mentors supplant women as figures of nurturance and sustenance, in addition to serving as male role models. This dialectic is important in the narrative of Davis's new life, and it also becomes an integral element of his future vision of creative, homosocial, musical collectivities.

In order to establish the dual function of his musical male mentors, Davis denies the maternal and nurturing function to his mother, Cleota H. Davis, and to other women. A constant refrain of *Miles* is the incompatibility of his life with women and his life in music, and he seeks to free himself from any claims that women might make upon him. In the early pages of the book Davis links his mother to fears of separation and absence in his childhood: "My mother was always . . . putting me, my brother, and my sister on trains when we were real young to go visit my grandfather." Cleota Davis was branded as one who failed to nurture. Though she gave her children food for their journeys, that didn't do any good: "that chicken was gone as soon as the train left the station. Then we'd starve all the way to wherever we were going. . . . We'd be crying all the way to my grandfather's house, hungry and mad."[13] As the narrative progresses, the mother is the primary figure her son associates with physical punishment; "my mother would whip the shit out of me at the drop of a hat," he recalls. But, even more significantly, his mother is a potential threat to the emerging definition of his own masculinity: she is the problem and she is the one who has a problem.

When Davis was thirteen, the trumpet was the reason for a dispute between his parents and, subsequently, the instrument acquired the symbolic qualities of manhood for Davis. Cleota wanted her son to have a violin and was overruled.

It was about that time that I first started having serious disagreements with my mother. Up until then, it had been over small things. But it just kind of went downhill. I don't really know what *her problem* was. But I think it had something to do with her not talking real straight to me. She was still trying to treat me like I was a little baby, the way she was treating my brother Vernon. I think this had something to do with him becoming a homosexual. The women—my mother, my sister, and my grandmother—always treated Vernon like a girl. So I wasn't having none of that shit from them.[14]

In the first two chapters of *Miles*, Cleota's failure to nurture the child, her refusal to allow him to grow, is elaborated into a wider female conspiracy to undermine social conventions of masculinity. The trum-

pet Davis gets as an adolescent becomes one important key in an elaborate strategy of opposition to femaleness, a strategy which he describes
as necessary to define his own code and definition of manhood. But at
the core of these definitions is Davis's homophobia. His ability to establish his own terms and conditions for maturing into a *real* man is contrasted to his brother's inability to remove himself from the influence
of women, thus allowing their "problems" to deform Vernon's masculinity.

After giving an account of how his musical career and manhood
began to develop among the men he admired, he returns to the mother
figure and reflects upon her physical and spiritual beauty. But she is
forever dissociated from what Davis wants to become in the manly
world of jazz. Cleota Davis, in her son's vision of his world, did not
produce and has no relation to the *man* he has become and, indeed, as
far as Davis is concerned, he becomes a man in spite of his mother and
the other women in his life.

Anxieties about women stunting his growth emerge in Davis's relationship with Irene Birth and their first daughter, Cheryl. While Davis
experienced a revelation of orgasmic proportions when he first heard
Dizzy Gillespie and Charlie Parker play when he was eighteen, his
description of his first orgasm with a woman is tinged with disgust for
her origins. Irene comes from a world with which he does not want to
be associated. Her neighborhood was not only poor and black but had a
"real bad smell in the air, of burnt meat and hair."[15] Such language
emphasizes his belief that women are a possible source of contamina-
tion. When Davis marries Irene and she gives birth to a girl, he comes
to resent his family responsibilities, because the time he has to spend
with them is time taken from his life as a musician. "And with Irene
home, well I had to be taking care of my husband duties with her
sometimes, you know, being with her, shit like that. Then Cheryl would
be crying. It was a motherfucker."[16] This scenario gets repeated in later
marriages and develops into a fundamental conflict:[17] when his home
life with a woman is going well, his musical life is going badly, and vice
versa.[18]

Davis's anger at his mother's supposed abandonment of him as a child constantly recurs in the narrative as a rage expressed in acts of violence against women. He recalls this brutality, without apparent regret, throughout *Miles*:

> I remember I hit [Frances Taylor] once when she came home and told me some shit about Quincy Jones being handsome. Before I realized what had happened, I had knocked her down. . . .
>
> We had our verbal arguments just like all couples have, but that was the first time I had hit her—though it wouldn't be the last. . . .
>
> I just wanted her with me *all* the time. But she would argue about that shit with me, tell me that she had a career, too, that she was an artist, too, but I just didn't want to hear no shit that was going to keep us apart. After a while, she stopped talking about it and started teaching a dance class for people like Diahann Carroll and Johnny Mathis. I didn't mind her doing that because she was home with me every night.[19]

In his account of his later marriage to Cicely Tyson, he coolly remembers how he "just slapped the shit out of her."[20]

In the early 1950s Davis becomes a pimp, using women to finance his heroin needs.[21]

> I was in a deep fog, high all the time and pimping women for money to support my habit through the rest of 1951 and the early part of 1952. At one time I had a whole stable of bitches out on the street for me. I was still living in and out of hotels. But it wasn't like people thought it was; these women wanted someone to be with and they liked being with me. I took them to dinner and shit like that. We'd get down on the sex thing, too, but that wasn't much, because heroin takes away your sex drive. I just treated the prostitutes like they were anybody else. I respected them and they would give me money to get off in return. The women thought I was handsome and for the first time in my life, I began to think I was too. We were more like a family than anything.[22]

Davis's inability or outright refusal to recognize that he exploited these women is integral to his view of himself in the situation he describes as being "like a family." While Davis is deeply resentful of his own family obligations toward Irene and his children, as master of a "stable" of women he can exercise apparently unlimited patriarchal power, as if it were his right and without demands being made upon him.[23]

To wield unlimited patriarchal power through control of sex workers was a desire that Davis shared with some of his peers in the jazz world. Charles Mingus, in his autobiography, makes explicit the connections between music, masculinity, and sex in an elaborate fantasy of the power he wanted to wield through his sound. "I could always hypnotize people. . . . I could hypnotize with music—they'd come running and screaming down the aisles and jumping out of bleachers. I wonder if I could hypnotize all the prostitutes of the world so they'd run into the streets nude to rape every man in sight! . . . Whores, off with the clothes of our leaders! . . . If they run cut off where their balls should be. Save this sick world, oh ye priceless whores!"[24] In Davis's account of the New York jazz scene, women are troublesome "bitches" that have to be managed: the relationships that black jazz musicians have with "white bitches," for example, are cited as the cause of "racial tension [among men] around bebop"; and "bitches" in general are mere sexual objects to be beaten when they step out of line.[25]

In this manner *Miles* puts women in their place and clarifies the use Davis will make of them. The true sources of nurturance, sustenance, and stimulation for his work are mutually fulfilling, male, and linked to performance; with them he interacts creatively, whereas women exist to be exploited and to service his bodily needs.

Pearl Cleage has publicly denounced Davis's violence against women and proposed a possible collective response.

I kept thinking about Cicely Tyson hiding in the basement of her house while the police were upstairs laughing with Miles. I wondered what she was thinking about, crouched down there in the darkness. I wondered if thinking about his genius made her less frightened and humiliated.

I wondered if his genius made it possible for her to forgive him for *self-confessed violent crimes against women such that we ought to break his records, burn his tapes and scratch up his CDs until he acknowledges and apologizes and agrees to rethink his position on The Woman Question. . . .*

I can't stop thinking about it. I can't stop wondering what we would do if the violence was against black men instead of black women. Would we forgive the perpetrator so quickly and allow him into our private time; our spiritual moments; our sweet surrenders?[26]

Cleage attempts to weigh, measure, and bring to account Davis's music in relation to what he does to the souls of black women—as much as the violence he perpetrates upon their bodies. I would like to explore the unfathomable space of this startling contradiction between the accomplishments of "genius" and the devastation rendered by patriarchal codes of domination.

I think it is very important to challenge the apparent distance between Davis's violence against women and the "genius" of his music, as if they were enacted on different planes of existence. First, this division reproduces the material/spiritual divide that Davis himself creates. The various women described in *Miles* are carefully given their place in his material world: they may service his bodily sexual and physical needs, but are albatrosses around his neck when he wants to fly with other men in the musical realm of "genius" and performance.

Of course, this characterization of women as weights that bring men down is directly contrary to the true history of women in the jazz world. As Val Wilmer, a jazz music journalist, has pointed out, "Most of the older musicians had a hard-working wife in the background that stuck with them," providing a stable income and material and spiritual sustenance. Said one such wife, "I think we become their mothers. We're like their support, we're there for them to fall back on, to throw their garbage on—to throw their good feelings on too."[27] Lorraine Gillespie makes eloquent testimony to her contribution to Dizzy Gillespie's success:

> When I met him, he was just as raggedy as a bowl of yat ko mein and as poor as a non-bearing beanpole. . . . I had to help him build this, this "empire" that he's living up on. The only part I didn't do was blow, but if I hadn't done what I did, he wouldn't have been blowing 'cause he wouldn't have had the strength to blow with. . . . I don't have the time to be worrying about what somebody else "thinks". . . . They don't worry about who's back there in the back sweeping the floor, and cleaning the garbage and all. . . . All they see is the smiling and Uncle Tomming and stuff. But they don't know what it takes to come to that, you know.[28]

To accept the division between the inspirational world of jazz music and the mundane world that includes women renders invisible the labor of women that have made the music possible at great cost to themselves.

Stories of how female jazz performers survived diverge dramatically according to the sex of the narrator. Dizzy Gillespie maintains that Sarah Vaughan's strategy in the Billy Eckstine Band was to become one of the boys.

> Sarah Vaughan acted just like one of the boys. She put herself in that position, one of the boys, just another musician, and she was as good a musician as anybody in the band. She could play the piano, knew all the chords, and played terrific chords behind us. I remember Ella never acted like one of the boys; she always played the role of a lady. But you could say anything you wanted to in front of "Sailor," uh, I mean, Sarah. She'd use the same language I used with the guys.[29]

Gillespie assumes that Vaughan made her own decisions about how to act and fails to acknowledge any limitations on her behavior or pressure from the rest of the band. Vaughan's own interpretation of her life in the band is somewhat different: "It was a very rough band. They kept me in order. I'm telling you they used to beat me to death if I got out of line. I mean, literally, kicked my what's-its-name. Oh, my Lord, my arm used to be so sore. But I would never do that again, whatever that was."[30]According to Vaughan, she had far less freedom to act than Gillespie grants her and suffered physical abuse if she stepped out of line.

As Leo Bersani has argued, "It is perhaps unfortunate, but no less true, that we have *learned to desire* from within the heterosexual norms and gendered structures that we can no longer think of as natural, or as exhausting all the options for self-identification."[31] Thinking from within these heterosexual norms, as Davis does, underlies these female-male, body-soul divisions and creates the split between the material world and the world of desire as opposing and autonomous forces.

It is the case that for both Davis and Delany, much of their lives has been "passed on society's margins," to use Delany's description.

I am attracted to those areas that most fiction handles with both textual and structural clichés—blacks, women, the mentally ill, the socially marginal, the relationship between society and sex—because I have had first hand experience with many of the situations they imply: I am black, I have spent time in a mental hospital, and much of my adult life, for both sexual and social reasons, has passed on society's margins. My attraction to them as subject matter for fiction, however, is not so much the desire to write autobiography, but the far more parochial desire to set matters straight where, if only one takes the evidence of the written word, all would seem confusion.[32]

Both men seek to "set matters straight" about lives spent in milieus which have been not only socially marginalized but rigorously policed: Davis as a black man who was also a jazz musician, and Delany as a black man who was also gay. In their autobiographies Davis and Delany add up the cost of living on the coercive edge of the social order and conclude that finding others like themselves is crucial to the formation of their own subjectivity. The naming or listing of these others is not just about mentoring or delineating complex strands of influence but is also a process of recognizing that others share, and most importantly survive, the destructive consequences of this marginality.

Jazz musicians claimed that booking agencies were run "like plantations."[33] Between 1926 and 1990, the cabaret laws of New York City branded "jazz music as deviant,"[34] and in 1940, "the police began to fingerprint every person who worked in a licensed place, and to issue identification cards, denying the cards to people they thought were not of good character." The issuing of cards was directed not only at musicians but at all employees of licensed cabarets, and it has been asserted that this was part of an intensifying campaign against radicals. However, these laws were also clearly racist in their effects, part of a wider "impulse to control the supposedly degrading abandon of black music."[35] Many musicians, including Thelonius Monk and Billie Holiday, had their cards taken away for some offense and spent years trying to get their cards back, while some were refused cards outright.

> To play jazz was to be a musical outsider, even sometimes a revolutionary, to cut against the grain of ordinary musical taste. The City's rules governing the lives of musicians, together with the nature of the places where the music was played, only exemplified, indeed legislated, that status. And many musicians lived the status, making it part of them. If they played complex and difficult music, and played it as they pleased, they paid the price for it. They rejected and were rejected by the "square" world.[36]

Davis's own cabaret license was revoked after an incident which illustrates how the policing of the supposed threat of black male sexuality meshed with the policing of the jazz and cabaret world.

Because Davis was in the company of a white woman, whom he was walking to her cab outside of the club in which he was performing, he was first harassed, then beaten, and finally arrested by the police.[37] After recounting this incident in *Miles*, Davis reflects upon two subsequent, opposing reactions toward him. Other musicians, both black and white, he says, regarded him as a hero for standing up to the police, but some "white people . . . started saying that I was always 'angry', that I was 'racist.' " Davis's response was to refuse to act submissive: "Now, I've been racist toward nobody, but that don't mean I'm going to take shit from a person just because he's white. I didn't grin or shuffle and didn't walk around with my finger up my ass begging for no handout and thinking I was inferior to whites. I was living in America too, and I was going to try to get everything that was coming to me."[38] Davis's reaction is very defensive, and it focuses on his determination to be included as an equal in society. He does not question how the society itself is constituted.

Delany's reaction to police harassment is much more complex and emphasizes the importance of the subversive potential of the marginalized existence in which he lives. He details the persistently aggressive intervention of the police into gay bars and clubs, but draws a different conclusion from Davis's claim of inclusion into the social order. In a memorable moment in *Motion of Light in Water*, Delany achieves a far deeper political recognition of the subversive potential of the homosexual world he has discovered. The first time he goes to the St. Marks Baths and enters the gym, he experiences "a kind of heart-thudding astonishment, very close to fear," at the scene of masses of naked male bodies engaged in sex.[39] He had felt such fear before: one night, Delany was approaching the truck park at the docks on Christopher Street, where up to a hundred and fifty men would use the trailers for sexual encounters, and a police raid began. It wasn't the raid that provoked the fear but "the sheer number of men who suddenly began to appear, most of them running, here and there from between the vans."[40]

The fear had been rooted in the "fifties model of homosexuality"— which was believed to be a "solitary perversion"—a model that controlled Delany's homosexual existence and the law that policed him. The newspapers only occasionally reported raids like the one on Christopher St., and when they did, would mention only very small numbers of men involved. Such media silence acted to reassure the public of the isolated nature of this "perversion." But from this phenomenon Delany draws an important political insight.

> Whether male, female, working or middle class, the first sense of political power comes from the apprehension of massed bodies. That I'd felt it and was frightened by it meant that others had felt it too. The myth said we, as isolated perverts, were only beings of desire, manifestations of the subject (yes, gone awry, turned from its true object, but, for all that, even more purely subjective).
>
> But what *this* experience said was that there was a population— not of individual homosexuals . . . not of hundreds, not of thousands, but rather of millions of gay men, and that history had, actively and already, created for us whole galleries of institutions, good and bad, to accommodate our sex.[41]

What Delany hopes is that "once the AIDS crisis is brought under control . . . the West will see a sexual revolution to make a laughing stock of any social movement that till now has borne the name."[42]

Delany's vision of the necessity for total social and political transformation is revolutionary, whereas Davis's is reformist. Davis represses what Delany expresses. Where Delany's radical vision leads him to explore the inequality in gendered power relations between men and women, Davis believes such relations are part of the natural order. What Delany reveals as the workings of ideology, Davis attempts to rationalize and justify, and what Delany exposes as an intolerable imposition of the state on individual and social freedom, Davis disguises as gender difference. But if we analyze Davis's innovations in jazz and assess the nature of his emotionally charged and passionate musical experiments, then we may find a more radical and, at times, revolutionary, challenge to the conventions of masculinity.

Samuel Delany's *Motion of Light in Water* is such an effective counterpoint to Davis's *Miles* because it is a magnificent attempt to reject the socially created obstacles separating desire from its material achievement, and in the process demolishing and transcending the limitations of heterosexual norms: "The parallel column containing the discourse of repetition, of desire, whether satisfied or unrequited (but always purveying its trope of truth), forever runs beside one of positive, commercial, material analysis. Many of us, raised on literature, have learned to supply the absent column when the material is presented alone. And a few of us have begun to ask, at least, for the column of objects, actions, economics, and material forces when presented only with, in whatever figurative form, desire."[43]

At times Delany literally creates multiple columns of writing that express relations between them. One of the most important figures in his work is a place called The Bridge of Lost Desire.[44] This bridge has multiple existences in the material world, carrying the streets of the city (of New York) and articulating the relationships between and among its parts. The Bridge of Lost Desire is a figurative and a literary device that serves not only to join two shores of existence but functions as a space in its own right, which must be entered and explored: a space within which the relation between the two shores is expressed and our subjectivities formed. As a writer, Delany consciously creates this bridge to enter this space with paper and pen. I want to argue that we can use this Bridge of Lost Desire to cross the space that separates the two mutually exclusive worlds out of which Davis's subjectivity is constituted. His music, particularly the album Cleage talks about in her essay, *Kind of Blue*, offers us, if not a resolution to this contradiction, then a possible alternative understanding of his representations of masculinity.[45]

Davis's attempt to kick heroin is accompanied by a change in his public style. In 1954, the figure who comes to dominate his life and, subsequently, the narrative of *Miles* is that of the boxer Sugar Ray Robinson, "the most important thing in my life besides music. I found myself even acting like him, you know, everything. Even taking on his arrogant attitude."[46] Besides being a model of "cool," of precision and discipline, Sugar Ray Robinson had a very close relationship with a man everyone referred to as "Soldier." "Soldier" was the only person Sugar Ray Robinson listened to, other than his trainer, and Davis decided that he needed a Soldier of his own. His Soldier would be a musical partner and confidant.

> Ray was cold and he was the best and he was everything I wanted to be in 1954. I had been disciplined when I first came to New York. All I had to do was go back to the way I had been before I got trapped in all that bullshit dope scene. So that's when I stopped listening to just anybody. I got myself a Soldier just like Sugar Ray had; and my man for talking to was Gil Evans. . . .
>
> Of all the people I knew, Gil Evans was one of the only ones who could pick up on what I was thinking musically. Like when he would come to hear me play, he would ease up next to me and say, "Miles, you know you got a nice open sound and tone on your trumpet. Why don't you use it more." And then he'd be gone, just like that, and I'd be left thinking about what he had said. I would decide right then and there that he was right. Or, he would come up and whisper—always confidentially, so no one else could hear— "Miles, now don't let them play that music by themselves. You play something over them, put your sound in it too."
>
> I . . . realized that a person is lucky if he's got *one* Soldier or Gil Evans in his life . . . who knows what I would have become if I hadn't had someone like Gil to remind me? . . . I just came back to myself and kept on trying to grow, which was what I was all about when I came to New York in the first place—growing.

I take this moment of self-conscious revision in *Miles* as prefigurative of his future performance strategies and male musical relationships.

The high level of intimacy and immediacy of the musical relationships that could be attained in jazz is attested to by other musicians. Charles Mingus recalls Lionel Hampton's belief that Mingus was capable of projecting his thoughts: "I said nothing, I just *thought*. Then Hamp said, 'You the weirdest cat I know, standing there looking innocent yet putting your thoughts over the whole band into my head.' "[47] Nat Hentoff has asserted that the one generalization that could be made about jazz and its musicians, who are usually regarded as unpredictable, is that "jazz offers its players more freedom to express who they are—at any moment—than any other form of Western music."[48] This kind of intimacy and relations of trust are reproduced in complex ways in the relations between Davis and his instrumentalists—they form a "bridge of lost desire" and directly contrast with his "self-confessed violent crimes against women."[49]

For a first instance in the discussion of musical relationships I refer to a recording of "Bags' Groove," made on December 24, 1954, which has become famous for a musical quarrel between Davis and the jazz pianist Thelonius Monk.[50] The session is well known for Davis's spoken request to Monk that he "lay out," stop playing, during his solos. Davis claimed that "he loved Monk's compositions and his unique approach to piano . . . [but that] he couldn't stand his eccentric accompaniment style."[51] As he explained it, "Monk never did know how to play behind a horn player. . . . Trumpets don't have that many notes, so you really have to push that rhythm section and that wasn't Monk's thing."[52] Davis felt Monk was not the sort of musical partner he needed, and it is interesting to speculate on the musical consequences of the decisions which informed Davis's musical leadership.

Jazz critics have noted that Thelonius Monk and Miles Davis had very different visions of the rhythm sections they liked to work with because of their distinctive patterns of phrasing. Monk's syncopation was irregular; some describe it as consistently placing his notes against the groove. As a leader, therefore, Monk had a "preference for a firm, even heavy rhythm team whose pulse is relatively explicit."[53] On the other hand, Davis has been regarded as "a melodist whose lyrical phrasing is inconsistent in the sense that during a given phrase some notes may fall behind the pulse, others ahead of it, still others directly on it. . . . He often tends to float around the groove rather than attack it directly . . . he needs a rhythm section that can swing well on its own."[54] However, if one listens to Monk's solo in this recording and contrasts it with the way Davis both precedes and follows him, the music will show how complex their differences were and offer an insight into how Davis formed his later ensembles.

Davis's and Monk's solos are virtuoso performances not in the least interdependent or interwoven with each other. Davis's first solo opens spaces, or silences, in the music that are an invitation to the other instrumentalists to follow. Milt Jackson on vibes accepts this challenge, but evens out his phrasing to such an extent that Davis's spaces are absorbed into his response. Monk's solo refuses the offer. His phrasing is completely distinctive, ignoring Davis's patterns rather than entering and completing them, and Monk creates his own structure of rhythm and interpretation. Their interpretations, Davis concluded, were incompatible.

In stark contrast, "'Round Midnight," recorded on September 10, 1956, almost two years later, demonstrates how a very different ensemble worked together. Gil Evans, Davis's "Soldier," wrote the arrangement for "'Round Midnight," and the recording both forecasts how their partnership was to develop, and how another instrumentalist, John Coltrane, on tenor saxophone, came to embody just what Davis wanted from a workable partnership.[55] The opening bars of "'Round Midnight" establish an extraordinary musical relationship between Coltrane and Davis. Coltrane uses all the spaces that Davis opens up, in a muted but firm series of phrases that wind their way in and out of Davis's notes. The tenor sax supports and anchors Davis's flights into the high notes, gently modulates his stretch, and emphasizes the ambition of his reach. Where Davis stretches, Coltrane slides across and underneath, leaving Paul Chambers on bass and "Philly Joe" Jones on drums to seal around the edges of the seamless pair at their center. By the time Coltrane's solo enters, he is sinuously working out the relationship already established with Davis in the opening, and at the moment when he moves to transcend the pattern, Davis's solo pulls Coltrane back to the beginning. As they close, Coltrane is almost reluctant, playing just behind Davis, and though their timing is just slightly different, they complete each other's melodic structure. (How different, how superior is this relationship to Davis's relationships with women, whom he accuses of weighing him down!)

Yet Davis could be as violent towards Coltrane as towards the women in his life. Thelonius Monk saw Davis slap Coltrane's face and punch him in the stomach, presumably about something Coltrane had or hadn't played, and Monk immediately told Coltrane he did not have to put up with such treatment and asked him to work with him. Coltrane did indeed leave Davis for the Thelonius Monk Quartet in the spring of 1957 but returned in November because, he said, Miles's music "gave [him] plenty of freedom" to play around with chords or to play melodically.[56]

I do not want to suggest that in this musical relationship Coltrane was placed in a subordinate position, nor reduce their musical and interpretive styles to a simplistic formulation of compatibility. Rather, I want to explore and define what Davis meant by "growth" at this particular period of his life, a musical growth enabled and nurtured by his musical partnerships with men. It is those frequently stark *differences* between Davis and Coltrane that brought forth that interdependent relationship of growth in the performance—a relationship which Jack Chambers, music critic and historian, has called "arranged dynamism" between the two musicians.[57]

This "arranged dynamism" is an essential element of what Davis means by growth. To my mind, the influence of Ahmad Jamal, the pianist, upon Davis, transposed into the dynamics of the arranged relation between Davis and Coltrane, was an integral part of this pattern of growth. As Davis so frequently said, "I wanted to hear space in the music . . . the concept of space breathing through the music . . . [a concept] that I had picked up from Ahmad Jamal."[58] Thelonius Monk could not provide that space, but Coltrane, so eloquently and fruitfully for their musical partnership, could. It is in this conceptual space, on this "bridge of lost desire," that the dynamic tension between Davis and Coltrane arises. It indicates the formation of a new musical relation which also produces, during the performance, alternative gendered meanings in their relationship as men. Their way of playing together suggests the possibilities of a new intimacy and interdependency, intensity and passion, among instrumentalists.

Samuel Delany has wondered, "*Is* it the easy stories that make us who we are? *Is* it what, when we can finally tell them, the hard stories reveal of us? Or is it simply the gap, the tension, the places where the two are always threatening to tear entirely apart, that finally mold us, at any moment, to a given response, active or internal, that make others—or even ourselves—recognize us as persons?"[59] It is precisely what happens on the bridge, in the set of relations that make up the almost tactile tension across the gap Delany describes, that we can learn about the musical story of Davis and Coltrane.

If we listen to the opening bars of Ahmad Jamal's version of the Rogers and Hammerstein song "Surrey with the Fringe on Top," and then listen to Davis and Coltrane's considered response, recorded in May 1956, we can hear this dynamic tension at work. Davis's solo in a more measured and leisurely manner extends Jamal's understatement of the melody and opens up even more space than Jamal himself had done. The muted trumpet is romantic, soft, erotic, and at times almost coy in its lingering hesitancy. Coltrane responds strongly. Jack Chambers has characterized Coltrane as coming "roaring in to take over in no uncertain terms," but I prefer the description that Amiri Baraka gives: "Miles's darting blue flashes and sometimes limpid lyricism were now placed in tandem collaboration with the big densely powerful song of Coltrane."[60] Coltrane maintains a dialogue with Jamal's pacing while he responds directly to Davis, addressing his voicings into the spaces of Davis's silence. The effect is a coherent structure of call and response, the muted call receives a dramatic, complex, and uncompromising response, and each is dependent upon the other for musical and emotional completion, and for conceptual closure.

The growth of this musical intimacy and interdependence among the instrumentalists of Davis's increasingly modal period created new musical avenues for the exploration and expression of emotions, but this intimacy and interdependence also created an unconventional, gendered vulnerability. Herbie Mann implies such feelings when he tells how he was inspired by Davis to make his flute into a jazz instrument. "The attraction of Miles to me as a flutist was that he could be masculine, could communicate strong feeling with his horn and still be subtle and rarely sound beyond the volume level of the flute. He proved you don't have to yell and scream on your instrument to project feeling."[61]

Such deepened feeling and the accompanying vulnerability vis-à-vis his instrumentalists is the source, I believe, of Davis's elaboration of strategies for increasing the distance between himself as performer, and his audience. Vulnerablity and interdependence in musical production were masked behind the screen of arrogance and disdain for the audience. Amiri Baraka has brought our attention to the aesthetic importance of this distance between audience and performer: "There is an element of pure 'mood music' in Miles, and even when he is cracking at his hottest or coolest, this aspect of his sensibility provides a *distance*, actually, making his voice apparently more clearly perceived, but actually creating an aesthetic distance, a sensuous alienation, that makes us think we can circumscribe all of the player/composer with our feelings."[62] This distance and apparent disdain, which became an integral element in the Davis myth, also had an ideological dimension and function. They act as a barrier between, on the one hand, the world of the men who were his musical colleagues and partners, those who shared in the mutual expression and cultural production of vulnerability and interdependence and, on the other hand, the world of women, perceived as a threatening realm of "bitches."

To see women as "bitches," to relegate them to a service role, and to treat them with violence was the way to forge the bridge of male intimacy and to protect it from the danger of being considered unmasculine in conventional terms. Both the denial of dependency upon women and the aggression toward them fostered the homosocial jazz world of creativity, just as in the wider world female labor supports and maintains the conditions for the production of male creativity.[63]

These musical performances should be regarded as gendered experiences both for performers and for their audience. As Raymond Williams has written: "Art cannot exist unless a working communication can be reached, and this communication is an activity in which both artist and spectator participate."[64] In music, one important medium for this communication is rhythm.

> We are only beginning to investigate this on any scientific basis, but it seems clear from what we already know that rhythm is a way of transmitting a description of experience, in such a way that the experience is re-created in the person receiving it, not merely as an "abstraction" or an "emotion" but as a physical effect on the organism—on the blood, on the breathing, on the physical patterns of the brain. . . . The dance of the body, the movement of the voice, the sounds of instruments are, like colors, forms and patterns, means of transmitting our experience in so powerful a way that the experience can be literally lived by others. This has been felt, again and again, in actual experience of the arts, and we are now beginning to see how and why it is more than a metaphor; it is a physical experience as real as any other.[65]

In music criticism this argument is not all that "clear," and it is certainly not accepted in the formalist approaches that dominate the field. But in trying to locate and evaluate the gendered nature of the musical experience, it is vital that we understand that "Music is a powerful social and political practice precisely because in drawing upon metaphors of physicality, it can cause listeners to experience their bodies in new ways."[66]

At the same time, I would like to distance myself from critics who have tried to make the relation between musical metaphor and physical experience by employing Freudian symbolism—horns as phallic objects—and promoting "a discourse of the phallus among jazz artists."[67] For this is not what I wish to accomplish. Jazz criticism that plays games of "spot the phallic symbol" is in my opinion, severely limited in its conceptual and explanatory power for feminists. How, for example, can phallic discourse describe the complexity of the musical relationship generated by Julian "Cannonball" Adderley, Coltrane, and Davis, as they walk a tightrope balancing their individual explorations of the theme in "Miles" (which became popularly known as "Milestones"), recorded on April 2, 1958?[68]

The album *Milestones*, critics generally agreed, was excitingly innovative, and the excitement is described in almost explicitly sexual terms, with overtones that sound traditionally heterosexual and patriarchal. To quote Ian Carr, the most significant aspects of the title track, for example,

> are the rhythms of the piece and the way the structure builds and releases tension. The written theme and its structure (which is rigorously preserved for each soloist) are a brilliant refashioning of the old call-and-response idea. The first sixteen bars are the "call," and they set up a superbly springy rhythmic pulse. Here Miles the composer, by using extremely simple devices with immense subtlety, has created an entirely fresh feel, a new rhythmic dynamism and springboard. The three horns play, in simple triads, a three note riff which moves up and down the scale. The notes are short, played with great precision, and don't fall on the fourth beat of any bar. The rhythm section plays a bright 4/4 and Philly Joe once more ticks off the last beat of every bar with a rimshot, thus providing a kind of punctuation for the horn riff. During the second sixteen bars, this buoyant pulse is interrupted and held back with great artistry, thus producing a feeling of slowing up, though the actual tempo remains the same. This impression is created because the bass, instead of "walking" purposefully up and down the scale playing [quarter notes], simply repeats pedal notes E and A, while Philly Joe's rimshot falls on different beats in the bar, thus stopping the regularity of the rhythm. The two saxophonists continue playing up and down the scale in harmony, but this time with longer notes [half-notes], while Miles plays . . . slightly out of phase with the saxes; his rising and falling notes are played *against* theirs, dragging the phrases back. The tension rises as all these factors pull against the memory of that first springy rhythm, and then suddenly the last eight bars arrive, the original beat is back, and the tension is released magnificently. . . . The effect of the piece depends on the

contrast between the passion [Miles's solo] generates and the immensely ancient modal quietude of its first statement.[69]

If music embodies but also produces the social values of its time, then this piece emphasizes the patriarchal and phallic aspects of the sexual, the creation and the release of tension.

Certainly, it takes no particularly active act of the imagination to hear the sensual, sexual, and phallic overtones in this description of the musical relation between saxophones and trumpet. Feelings of pleasure and desire are aroused by the way the sounds of the saxophones and the trumpet respond to each other, caress, stimulate, and excite each other. But in sexual-political terms, surely this must be recognized as homoerotic? The build-up of tension, the pleasure of anticipation and promise held back when Davis plays against Adderley and Coltrane, its release and the final rush which returns us to the ground of the first theme, yet slightly slower as if we were spent, create a physical, emotional, and intellectual response in the bodies of the musicians and the listeners—the invention of "mood," however, is built on a foundation of gendered social and political *meaning.*

Davis has been recognized for "his rare capacity to fuse a unit into an organically integrated whole," and this can clearly be heard in "Milestones."[70] But if, as feminists, we interrogate the homosocial politics of masculinity at play in this music, it seems clear that such sensuality, while homoerotic, remains phallocentric. The mood of this musical performance is analogous to the mood of phallocentric eroticism created by Samuel Delany when he describes the homosexual encounters near the waterfront on Christopher Street in New York. What is so uncanny about the parallel between the literary and musical language and the cultural production of gendered meanings in both, is the way in which the orgiastic is produced through an order that retains qualities of spontaneity and improvisation.

Sometimes to walk between the vans and cabs was to amble from single sexual encounter—with five, twelve, forty minutes between—to single sexual encounter. At other times to step between the waist-high tires and make your way between the smooth or ribbed walls was to invade a space at a libidinal saturation impossible to describe to someone who has not known it. Any number of pornographic filmmakers, gay and straight, have tried to portray something like it—now for homosexuality, now for heterosexuality—and failed because what they were trying to show was wild, abandoned, beyond the edge of control, whereas the actuality of such a situation, with thirty-five, fifty, a hundred all-but-strangers is hugely ordered, highly social, attentive, silent, and grounded in a certain care, if not community. At those times, within those van-walled alleys, now between the trucks, now in the back of the open-loaders, cock passed from mouth to mouth to hand to ass to mouth without ever breaking contact with other flesh for more than seconds; mouth, hand, ass passed over what ever you held out to them, sans interstice; when one cock left, finding a replacement—mouth, rectum, another cock—required moving only the head, the hip, the hand no more than an inch, three inches.[71]

Though silent, this literary scene produces a strong sense of creative orchestration of the interdependent and intimate phallocentric relation that exists between Davis and his instrumentalists in their performance of *Milestones* and later recordings. An interesting anecdote reproduced in *Miles* can elaborate this analogy.

When Bill Evans—we sometimes called him Moe—first got with the band, he was so quiet, man. One day, just to see what he could do, I told him, "Bill, you know what you have to do, don't you, to be in this band?"

He looked at me all puzzled and shit and shook his head and said, "No Miles, what do I have to do?"

I said, "Bill, now you know we all brothers and shit and everybody's in this thing together and so what I came up with for you is that you got to make it with everybody, you know what I mean? You got to fuck the band." Now I was kidding, but Bill was real serious, like Trane.

He thought about it for about fifteen minutes and then came back and told me, "Miles, I thought about what you said and I just can't do it, I just can't do that. I'd like to please everyone and make everyone happy here, but I just can't do that."[72]

Behind the joke here the figurative dimensions of homosociality remain: the ways in which the musical relationships between the members of this band were analogous to "fucking each other" and analogous too to Samuel Delany's orgiastic need to be acknowledged. Bill Evans, like Coltrane, was viewed by Davis as a perfect musical partner, another musician who could "play a little like that Ahmad thing, too."[73]

The ability of jazz music to subvert dominant understandings of masculinity came to full fruition in the album *Kind of Blue*, evident in the musical relationship among Davis, Coltrane, Adderley, Evans, Paul Chambers and James Cobb. Critics have recognized that *Kind of Blue* was a "seminal recording in the history of American music," but it is also significant for what it represents in male musical partnerships, "offering the soloists unprecedented improvisational freedom and minimal chordal restrictions."[74] The music registers a distinct movement away from the phallocentricity of mood and meaning in *Milestones* to an intimacy and passion of a very different form.

Bill Evans compared the album to a "Japanese visual art in which the artist is forced to be spontaneous. He must paint on a thin stretched parchment . . . in such a way that an unnatural or interrupted stroke will destroy the line or break through the parchment," and this is certainly an accurate description of its subtlety and discipline.[75] Recall Delany's using the space between two parallel columns of different texts to produce a new subject; this figure too is like the image of the multiple strokes that are drawn across the stretched parchment; and like the image created in the title of Delany's autobiography, *The Motion of Light in Water*. All three are applicable to the variety of "blues" in this album and the ebbing and flowing between them.

Delany asks us to "Consider two accounts of a life." Instead, I will ask you to consider the different strains of music that come from each instrumentalist in *Kind of Blue*. Still in Delany's words, note "the gap between them, the split, the flickering correlations between, as evanescent as light-shot water, as insubstantial as moonstruck cloud, are really all that constitutes the subject: not the content, if you will, but the relationships that can be drawn out of that content, and which finally that content can be analyzed down into."[76] *Kind of Blue* is an amalgam of such correlations across a spatial plane, a figure that Joe Henderson also evokes in the title of his tribute to Davis, *So Near, So Far: Musings for Miles.*[77] The performance of *Kind of Blue* is the sum of its musical relations and partnerships, which form and reform like Delany's "light-shot water."

The democratic nature of instrumental participation in the performance of *Kind of Blue* taken as a whole is striking. The album is framed by "So What" (track one) and "Flamenco Sketches" (track five). The first notes to be heard are from Paul Chambers, on bass, who enters not as backing, not as part of the rhythm section, but as a very tentative introduction to the melody. Chambers's first three notes of "So What" fall, as if tripping over each other, directly into the arms of Evans's three supporting chords on the piano, and the pattern is repeated as if Evans were needed as a place on which Chambers can land. The final track also opens with a pattern of bass notes from Chambers, to which Evans responds directly. Between the opening and closing compositions, instrumentalists take it in turns to open each piece and play off each other in a variety of ways. The second track, "Freddie Freeloader," is opened by Adderley and Coltrane supported by James Cobb on drums; the third track, "Blue in Green," is opened by Evans; and the fourth, "All Blues," is opened by Cobb, Chambers, and Evans, who are joined in a rhythmic pulse by Adderley and Coltrane, after which Davis enters, making it a collective journey through the theme.

The type of partnership that had opened up between Davis and Coltrane is elaborated and extended to include all instrumentalists, so that each individual composition embodies simplicity in its formal structure but allows for modal complexity in performance. After the opening pattern of "So What," Evans and Chambers join in an exploration which alternately ascends and descends through the scale. The bass initially calls to the piano; it responds, followed by the drums and finally joined by the saxophones. The bass takes the rhythmic and thematic lead, which is eventually handed over to Davis's trumpet solo. Coltrane's tenor solo explores both the heights of Chambers and Evans's ascent and the depths of their descent. In its structure, "So What" has a seemingly endless variety of patterning and sets the tone of the album, which consistently refuses closure.

"Freddie Freeloader" begins where "So What" almost ends, but this time the blues groundwork is laid by the saxophones of Coltrane and Adderley for Wynton Kelly's piano solo. Coltrane and Adderley are supported by Cobb and beckoned into the theme by Kelly. After a solo by Kelly and then by Davis, Coltrane enters to stretch the reach of each note to the utmost of its elasticity and to the limit of the tenor saxophone's register. Adderley's alto solo returns us to the blues theme of the album and redirects our attention toward another inconclusive ending.

"Blue in Green," as Bill Evans himself described it, extends into "a ten measure circular form . . . played by soloists in various augmentation and diminution of time values."[78] Its very circularity gives the appearance of a self-conscious and experimental exploration of the refusal of closure in "So What" and "Freddie Freeloader." After the four-measure introduction by Evans comes Davis's solo, exploring the scale in directions at times anticipated by and at others followed by Evans, who now and then provides a platform on which Davis's eighth notes can come to rest. Davis frequently lingers just behind Evans, entering almost late to pursue the haunting theme (a strategy he later returned to in his relationship with Herbie Hancock). Davis's flights are launched by Cobb and Chambers. Evans provides the bridge between Davis and Coltrane, who elaborates upon and embellishes Davis's solo, and returns us from Coltrane to Davis with a rich rhythmic improvisation upon Coltrane's melodic figures. In the musical relationship a very interesting ambiguity develops. Evans completes what Coltrane merely suggests and then Davis develops what Evans only hints at. There is extraordinary empathy and trust demonstrated in the relationship between these three. But at the end Evans is engaged only with Chambers; together they stitch their own interpretation through the composition, taking us through the figure once more but leaving it *unresolved* as if it could rework itself continuously.

The erotic pulse of "All Blues" works on the listener as the saxophones stroke the notes that flow out of each and out of the drums and bass. Davis's trumpet enters and sinuously weaves its way in and out and over the sensuous rhythm. A strongly syncopated change of pace is called back by Davis, but Evans continues to emphasize the off beats of Davis as Cobb insinuates himself between the two of them, then, dramatically, all three are seamlessly together. The rhythm section works across both saxophone solos in a complex series of time signatures and eventually returns to the initial rhythmic structure. Davis's trumpet urges all other instruments to follow, as if he were the Pied Piper, and the piece fades in another refusal to end.

After the opening of Chambers and Evans, Davis explores the haunting refrains and lonely flights which establish the dimensions of "Flamenco Sketches." In this composition Davis's flats are given greater depth than anywhere else on the album, prefiguring his work with Gil Evans on *Sketches of Spain*. Coltrane's solo pushes to be bolder than the consistent restraint of Evans, whereas Adderley's solo decisively nudges and pushes at Evans's heels. Evans's response is to linger, almost reluctantly, as he stays slightly behind Chambers and Cobb. Evans holds back behind the bass and drums and refuses to complete the theme, but together the three repeat the figures which introduce Davis's second solo. Remarkably, Davis achieves even greater quietude than did Evans's restraint. At the end of the piece Davis's contribution is so laid back that it just melds into the whole as if afraid to disturb what is already in place.

It is the very circularity and refusal to resolve the tension through any single climax in the album that poses a significant challenge to musical phallocentricity. *Kind of Blue* offers up a more revolutionary mode of being and understanding in its democratic sensibility. Through rhythm and movement it is open, vulnerable, and haunting with images of creative regeneration. The relations of performance between the instrumentalists defy any simple definitions of a sextet, as they are at times an amalgam of pairs, trios, and quartets in varying combinations of personnel within the sextet.[79] The intimacy, interdependence, and apparently endless variation and spontaneity under Davis's leadership is evident not only in *Kind of Blue* but can be traced across performances of any one particular composition.[80]

Davis's music provides numerous and contradictory examples of a gendered organizational structure that could be used to challenge jazz criticism by engaging with the sexual politics that inform and shape as well as give expression to the formal structures and performance of jazz music. As Robert Walser has argued, "accounting for [Davis's] success as a performer may require rethinking some of our assumptions about what and how music means."[81] Davis's life, his work, and the musical risks he took represent and recreate the contradictory sexual politics of the different historical moments through which he lived and produced.

But the ambiguity and complexity of the creative process that challenged gendered social conventions remained, for Davis, bound securely within the realm of his music. While Davis's ensembles were his creative alternative to destructive relationships with women, Delany applied his creativity to transcending the oppressive nature of the family, for men and women alike, with political force and commitment that go far beyond his writing.[82] In response to an interviewer who asked Delany why he chose to write science fiction, the writer responded by situating his own work in relation to writers who preceded him, those who were "developing a new way of reading, a new way of making texts make sense—collectively producing a new set of codes. And they did it . . . by writing new kinds of sentences, and embedding them in contexts in which those sentences were readable . . . a new way of reading *is* serious business."[83] As Delany's work charges his readers to accept the challenge of developing a new way of reading, so Davis's music should force us to develop new ways of listening.

I never hear the ball
slap the backboard. I slam it
through the net. The crowd goes wild
for our win. I scored
thirty-two points this game
and they love me for it.
Everyone hollering
is a friend tonight.
But there are towns,
certain neighborhoods
where I'd be hard pressed
to hear them cheer
if I move on the block.

ESSEX HEMPHILL

6

LETHAL WEAPONS
AND CITY GAMES

I'm an innocent bystander . . .
Send lawyers, guns and money
The shit has hit the fan.

Warren Zevon

As *Grand Canyon* opens, a blank screen is all that can be seen. Out of
the darkness gradually comes the pulsating sound of chopper blades.[1]
Like so many others of my generation, I am used to connecting this
sweep of mechanical wings with a particular place and history because,
for more than twenty years, the sound of low-flying helicopters was
used by film and television studios to signify the presence of Americans
in the war zones of Southeast Asia.

Peter Markle used exactly the same cinematic effect, a blank screen
and steady beat of helicopter blades, as the opening sequence of his
1988 Vietnam film, *Bat 21*.[2] By borrowing the opening of *Bat 21* for
Grand Canyon in 1991, director Lawrence Kasdan brings the Vietnam
war to the city of Los Angeles.[3] The strategy employed by Kasdan and
other Hollywood filmmakers to equate these particular killing fields
with the streets of Los Angeles is complex and contradictory and will
haunt this chapter. The dramatic effect, however, is startling. Although

ignorant of the subject of *Grand Canyon* when I started to watch it, the unmistakable sound of those blades alerted me to expect, post-Vietnam, the symbolic landscape of a black urban neighborhood.

Throughout the 1980s, Southeast Asia was presented in the popular culture of the United States as *the* primary site of the national nightmare: a landscape through which North American men crept under the constant surveillance of a subhuman population of menacing "gooks." The "enemy" masqueraded as ordinary men, women, and children by day but, within the heart of the nightmare, these people were never ordinary, never innocent, and barely human. Since then, this vision has been supplanted in the popular cultural and political imagination by images of black inner-city neighborhoods.

For contemporary Hollywood filmmakers, the black neighborhoods of Los Angeles have become important sites not just for the representation of death and destruction but for the enactment of racialized social and political confrontations that to them constitute a national crisis. Indeed, these neighborhoods are now, for bankers and studios alike, as fascinating in their exoticism, their potential for violent masculine confrontations, and therefore their commercial marketability, as was Vietnam. These neighborhoods have become the sites for the current enactment of the national nightmares of the white suburban bourgeoisie—these nightmares which are inscribed upon the bodies of young, urban black males and patrolled by the "Bloods" and the "Crips."

I am intrigued by Kasdan's *Grand Canyon* because it exemplifies Hollywood's fascination with the black inner city as the symbolic space of suburban anxiety. No matter how multiracial and multicultural our inner-city neighborhoods actually are, they are reduced in most Hollywood movies to an essentialist terrain of black and white male confrontation and resolution.

Grand Canyon conceals through its plot how, in a general way, it encourages white fear of black aggression. On the surface, the film appears merely to confirm what its target audience already understands, the material reality of the threat from young black men. But *Grand*

Canyon also creates a utopian and somewhat magical racial relationship between two mature men, one black, one white, which acts as a possible imaginative resolution to the fears and anxieties of white suburban residents. The promotional material which accompanies the home video describes it as follows: "*Grand Canyon* is director Lawrence Kasdan's powerful and uplifting film about real life and real miracles . . . and about how, after the millions of choices we make in life, one chance encounter can change it all."[4]

At the beginning of the film Mack, an immigration lawyer played by Kevin Kline, looks for a way to avoid the heavy traffic leaving the Los Angeles Forum after a Lakers' game. He strays into a black neighborhood that is so alien to him that he will later categorically assure his family, "You have *never been* where I broke down."[5] What happens to Mack is evocative of the modernist journey into the "heart of darkness," a journey originally conceived in the context of European imperialism in Joseph Conrad's novel of that name, and recreated by Hollywood in Francis Ford Coppola's postmodern fantasy of war in Southeast Asia, *Apocalypse Now.* As Mack peers anxiously out of his windscreen at the unfamiliar and, to him, menacing black residential neighborhood, Warren Zevon's music plays in his car.

Music is important to Kasdan, and the Warren Zevon soundtrack, "Lawyers, Guns, and Money," establishes a background for his protagonist. Clearly, the repetition of the plea to "send lawyers, guns, and money" increases the tension of the moment and emphasizes the risk of imminent danger, but the song also acts to situate Mack in history. Zevon's music is a product of the seventies, of white, yuppie, southern California culture. Mack's familiarity with the words and apparent nostalgia for the song places him within the liberal politics and culture of this time. The music provides the character with a social location and particular history.[6] Kasdan also uses music to signal the distance between modernist conceptions of history and subjectivity, such as those at work in Conrad's novel, and his own postmodern vision of the fragmentation of social and political positionality. In Kasdan's editing room the Zevon soundtrack was integrated into the film not only in order to register with the audience the potential threat to his protagonist but to prepare them for his making music the very ground of social and political conflict.

The words of "Lawyers, Guns, and Money" evoke, with a wry liberal irony, memories of the Cold War, of danger to Americans trespassing in exotic locales, and of covert intervention in other countries. The song also establishes the liberal credentials of the character of Mack, creates a mood of empathy for his mistake (his drive is intercut with scenes from the family home, complete with beautiful wife and handsome teenage son—all this he stands to lose), and alerts the audience to the gravity of his situation. As Mack's anxiety grows, Kasdan multiplies his visual and aural strategies for creating and maintaining anxiety, and increasing the sense of panic and foreboding in his audience.

Mack abruptly switches off his stereo in order to concentrate more effectively on finding his way home and, like a mouse in a laboratory maze, turns his car around in a futile effort to escape.[7] As Mack drives ever closer toward the "horror" that awaits, he passes the shells of cars and the skeletons of abandoned buildings. The landscape he drives through increasingly resembles a war zone, and Mack begins to sing Zevon's words himself as if to seek comfort in their meaning. But, as Mack mutters "send lawyers, guns, and money," his words are overwhelmed by the taunting voice of Ice Cube, "ruthless, plenty of that and much more," emanating from a white BMW that slows down and drives beside him like an animal stalking its prey. At this moment music becomes *the* prime vehicle for representing a cultural war which has encoded within it the political potential for a larger civil war. The rap group NWA (Niggaz with Attitude) is pitted against Zevon in a symbolic enactment of Kasdan's narrative of race and nation which is about to unfold: a liberal white suburban male confronts a "posse" of young black urban males. The musical battle both produces and accompanies the wider class and racialized meanings of the scene, meanings which in turn both produce and confirm contemporary ideological beliefs about the "problem" of the inner city, of what is wrong with America.

The skewed perspective of this cinematic confrontation is revealed in the unequal editing of the musical "war." In contrast to the verbal and musical fragments of NWA's "Quiet on the Set," the audience hears coherent narrative selections from the Zevon lyrics. We do not hear sequential sections of a verse, or even complete sentences, of the NWA lyrics; the narrative coherence of "Quiet on the Set" has been deliberately disrupted. The voice of Ice Cube fades in and out of the cat-and-mouse game as it is played out on the screen, and the words we can make out, "ruthless, plenty of that and much more," are intended only to confirm the menacing intentions of the occupants of the BMW, five young black males who take careful note of the interloper in their territory.

Mack responds to their presence by singing:

> I'm an innocent bystander . . .
> Send lawyers, guns and money
> The shit has hit the fan.

His car coughs, splutters, stalls, and finally stops, and Mack becomes a man under siege. He uses his car phone in a desperate attempt to get help, but isn't sure just where he is. "I dunno . . . let's say . . . Inglewood," he decides, without conviction, as the car phone itself crackles and dies. Having run to a public telephone outside a convenience store, Mack continues to find it difficult, if not impossible, to describe his location exactly or, to continue the military analogy, to give his coordinates. "Buckingham, yes," he pants, "but remember it's about half a mile West, I guess, of there." Mack is not only lost; he is in alien territory, and his very survival is at stake.

Kasdan carefully and deliberately recreates film narratives of Vietnam for his narrative of Los Angeles. Here again, he appears to be influenced by Markle's *Bat 21*, in which Gene Hackman finds himself alone in enemy territory. In that movie Hackman plays the part of a man who shouldn't be in the situation in which he finds himself; he is a missile intelligence expert who has had to bail out from an unarmed plane on a reconnaissance mission. His only chance of survival is at the other end of his communications device and depends upon providing his exact coordinates. The camera work of these parallel scenes, in which Hackman and Kline run and hide from their enemies, desperate to find a safe place from which to call for help, is too similar to be coincidental, but, even more importantly, the Vietnam narrative is present in Kasdan's decision to cast the same actor to play the part of the heroic rescuer.

Roadside assistance tells Mack that it will take forty-five minutes to get to him. He replies that he understands but warns, "if it takes that long I might be like, ah, dead." (In the Vietnam movie, the Hackman character is also told that it is not possible to send help straight away and has a similar reaction.) Both Hackman and Kline remain under enemy surveillance. In *Grand Canyon* the NWA soundtrack changes to include fragments of "F*** the Police," signifying the imminence of the moment of confrontation. Mack returns to his car to wait for help and the BMW pulls up behind him.

What follows is a filmic moment in which language, sound, and image coalesce to evoke intense emotions of danger and fear in the audience, reminding it of the feelings of an American soldier coming down in enemy territory. Through his personal distress Mack gives voice to the anxieties of a constituency of the white suburban middle class, whose greatest fear is being stranded in a black urban neighborhood at night. The young black men advance, framed by the rear windscreen. The camera then focuses on Mack's face. His eyes, seen in the rearview mirror, flicker as he breathes a final distress call: "Mayday, Mayday. We're coming down."

What Kasdan excludes from his audience in this scene is an irony that only those who know the lyrics of "Quiet on the Set" and "F*** the Police" would perceive. In fact, I would argue that Kasdan depends upon the ignorance of his target audience. For those who aren't familiar with the album *Straight Outta Compton*, "Quiet on the Set" is about the power of performance, specifically, the potential power that a successful rap artist can gain over his audience.[8] Power is, quite explicitly, the power of words over the body. For example, "ruthless, plenty of that and much more" is about controlling the movements of people, particularly women, on a dance floor, and about the power to create "a look that keeps you staring and wondering why I'm invincible." This invincibility is entirely the result of being able to persuade with words: "when you hear my rhyme its convinceable." Kasdan, however, disrupts NWA's intended narrative structure and lines like "I'm a walking threat" and "I wanna earn respect" are used to reinforce a contemporary image of the disobedient and dangerous black male who believes that respect is only gained through the possession of a gun (this is spelled out at the end of the confrontation). Perhaps the greatest irony of all is that the NWA song even predicts such misinterpretation and misuse of their words. Near the end of the rap, in a section excised from the film, an interesting dialogue occurs between Ice Cube and an unidentified voice that mimics the supposedly dispassionate, analytic tone of the sociologist or ethnographer. Ice Cube asserts that he can create "lyrics to make everybody say," and the academic voice responds: "They can be cold and ruthless, there's no doubt about that but, sometimes, it's more complicated." Ice Cube concludes: "You think I'm committing a crime, instead of making a rhyme."

A tow-truck driver comes to Mack's rescue at the height of his confrontation with the "gang" (in a similar way, in the rescue scene in *Bat 21*, a flyer heads toward Hackman at the last moment). Mack has been forced out of the safety of his car and is being directly threatened, when a blaze of oncoming headlights announces that he will be saved. The camera tantalizes the audience as it hesitates to reveal the identity of the man who climbs out of the truck. The lens tracks from the truck to Mack, flanked by the young black men in various poses of aggression, and then back again to the tow-truck driver's boots and slowly pans upwards. Here Kasdan reproduces the same low-angled shot he used moments before to stress the menacing nature of the black male faces that lean toward Mack in his car, a shot identical to one used in *Bat 21* as Hackman cowers away from the feet and legs of passing Viet Cong. Mack's rescuer is revealed to be a black man, armed with an enormous steel crowbar, a possible weapon, the size of which is exaggerated by the low camera angle. Before the audience can fully identify him, however, the tow-truck driver bends into the cab to reach for a cap.

This moment of uncertainty places in doubt the possible allegiance of the driver: is he really there to rescue Mack, as is implied by the change in the music, a signal upon which the audience has come to rely as a measure of mood? Or is the arrival of yet another black man an additional menace, as implied by the lingering of the camera over a body whose identity it is reluctant to reveal? The hesitation is only momentary, but it is sufficient to register ambiguity and doubt. Once the figure is revealed to be that of the actor, Danny Glover, the final threads of the complex Vietnam/Los Angeles web are woven in place. For Glover carries with him a built-in reference system from his previous roles, a filmic genealogy, if you will, that resolves any hesitation on the part of the audience about his possible allegiance. Indeed, Kasdan can toy so successfully with the audience's expectations because he can rely on the fact that Glover's appearance will instantly produce both the recognition and the assurance that he is a "good guy," a good black man:[9] after all, he was the heroic flyer who rescued Gene Hackman in *Bat 21* and the L.A.P.D.'s stalwart Sgt. Roger Murtaugh, whose partnership with Mel Gibson, in *Lethal Weapon*, has become a very profitable Hollywood legend.

The figure of Danny Glover as the tow-truck driver, Simon, is an important mechanism for the movie's resolution of the dilemma inherent in one of our most dominant contemporary narratives—a dilemma captured in the cinematic hesitation I have already described—how, exactly, can the white middle class distinguish between the good and the bad black male? The moment of Mack's rescue is a good point at which to interrupt the action in order to speculate about Kasdan's manipulation of black masculinity in his choice of Glover to play Simon.[10] It is through an analysis of the multiple ways in which the "good guy" genealogy has been formulated and established for Glover, a genealogy which film directors know exists in the popular imagination, that we can observe a particular narrative of race, nation, and masculinity at work.

Danny Glover's cinematic career blossomed during the conservative years of Reaganism and Reaganomics, but the particular projection of black manhood that Glover has come to embody is anticipated in interesting ways by the actor Canada Lee. In 1947, in Robert Rossen's *Body and Soul*, Canada Lee stars with John Garfield in a film about the corruption and violence present in the boxing world.[11] Garfield plays the part of a young and talented challenger to the title of world champion held by Ben Chaplin (Canada Lee). Both boxers are virtually owned by a gambler and boxing financier called Roberts, played by Lloyd Goff, who betrays Chaplin when it is profitable for him to do so. Chaplin is severely injured in a fight which leaves him with a blood clot on his brain. While encouraging Chaplin to fight Davis, assuring him that Davis will go easy on him, Roberts tells Davis, who remains ignorant of Chaplin's injury, to be brutal. When Chaplin is roughly defeated by Davis he is rushed to a hospital, and Davis discovers Roberts's betrayal. Contrite, Charlie Davis employs Ben Chaplin as his trainer, but Ben becomes much more: he becomes a voice of wisdom, an adviser, and a friend who, in contrast to Roberts, always has Charlie's interests at heart. He is not only a black man defeated and in a servile role; he is also proud, independent, and occupies the moral high ground. Chaplin is the only incorruptible man in the film, and when he dies, it is only his body that has gone; the moral and ethical superiority of his soul increases in power. In a number of scenes saturated by the music of "Body and Soul," Davis is finally persuaded to live up to the example of Ben Chaplin. When the ethical soul of the black man enters the white man's body, it ensures a return to honesty, integrity, and the familial social order.

This type of black male-white male partnership returns during the Reagan years, a period in which the partnership is elaborated into a complex social, political, and emotional as well as ethical unit. In *Bat 21*, Danny Glover's voice and his words of wisdom and advice are crucial to the eventual survival of the man he has to rescue. Like the character played by Canada Lee, Glover becomes obsessed with saving Hackman. He returns to fly over his position constantly, night and day, to the point of exhaustion and potential sacrifice of his own life. The words spoken by Glover through the radio become a literal lifeline, offering comfort against feelings of vulnerability and bringing encouragement, warmth, and hope to counter Hackman's despair. Again, like Canada Lee, Glover is portrayed as the man who can help the hero save himself from his enemies and, most importantly, save himself from his own weaknesses and fears. Danny Glover's film performances are a very significant elaboration of this portrayal of black manhood and constitute a complex, if contradictory, referential history of contemporary meanings of race and masculinity .

Danny Glover made his first movie appearance in the 1979 *Escape from Alcatraz*, in which he played one of many anonymous black male convicts.[12] In 1981 he was cast in *Chu Chu and the Philly Flash* as a member of a group of homeless men and women who lived in San Francisco's ferry terminal.[13] In this screwball comedy, Glover's black masculinity is rendered harmless as he forms part of an inept team whose antics resemble those of the Keystone Cops. The following year Glover appeared in the avant garde film *Out!*, aka *Deadly Drifter*.[14] Though in *Out!* Glover has the part of an urban revolutionary, complete with black leather coat and a stick of dynamite, he is not cast as a member of a threateningly dangerous black revolutionary army. On the contrary, Glover is, again, the only black member of a white collective and, toward the end of the film, is partnered with Peter Coyote in a mildly comic relationship. The film is an absurdist dismantling of revolutionary aims and methods through an existential journey across the United States. The desire for revolution is transformed into a New Age meditation on the moral and ethical superiority of native peoples and whales.

In 1984, however, Glover moves away from the syndrome of black male as criminal/outcast in his role of a laboratory assistant, Loomis, in Fred Schepisi's *Iceman*.[15] Though Loomis is a minor role, this is Glover's first opportunity to perform the part of a black male with a heart. The Iceman is a Neanderthal found frozen in the ice and brought back to life by a team of scientists; he is then kept under observation in an artificial habitat as if he were a specimen in a cage. In a brief but significant scene, the Glover character allies himself with the people who condemn this captivity on moral grounds and unlocks the door to let the Iceman escape, thus prefiguring his many later roles as a savior.

The role of Mose in Robert Benton's *Places in the Heart*, 1984, provides one of the keys to the development of Glover's cinematic genealogy as a good, trustworthy black man.[16] At the beginning of *Places in the Heart*, set in Texas in 1935 at the height of the Depression, Mose is a hobo and petty thief who steals the silver of a newly widowed young woman (Sally Field) while claiming to be looking for work. Field's husband and provider, the town sheriff, has recently been shot and killed by a drunken young black man, so the threat to the white family from lawless black men has multiple dimensions. Indeed, Glover's character could be described as a "deadly drifter," one who steals what little of value is owned by Field and her children, who are struggling to keep their farm from falling into the hands of a bank that wants to foreclose on its mortgage. When the thief is arrested, however, and returned to her house for identification, Field lies, claiming that Mose carries her silver with her permission in order to sell it for her. This generous action transforms the black man into an absolutely loyal bondsman and deliverer of a white family. This loyalty is supplemented by seemingly unlimited expressions of sacrifice and nobility, as Mose works to save the family in spite of tremendous opposition. He becomes their archetypal male provider, savior, and defender against all threats from the institutional forces of the dominant society, represented by the Bank and the Cotton Gin.

However, while Mose can successfully perform as the brains and the brawn hidden behind the skirts of a white woman, he fails to establish his patriarchal equality as a black man confronting white men. When threatened by the manager of the bank and the owner of the cotton gin, in their guise as leaders of the local Klan, Mose is forced to flee for his life. Ultimately, the black male ends as he began, without a place in this community—a figure of nobility but apart. In addition, the sense of worth of the black man is not gained through self-knowledge or self-respect but is granted from the outside. Mose's black masculinity gains its masculinity, as humanity, through white recognition: in the closing moments of the film, before he has to leave the town forever, Field acts like a queen bestowing a knighthood when she acknowledges Mose's loyalty and achievements: "Remember, you did this." It is this act of acknowledgment that remains with the character of Mose (and the audience). In the absence of a reward in the form of material goods, profit, or a social role in the community, these words are meant to sustain and comfort Mose. Recognition is his only consolation for his necessary racial exclusion from the family and the community for whose survival he is responsible.

In this sense, the resolution of *Places in the Heart* reproduces the resolution of Harriet Beecher Stowe's *Uncle Tom's Cabin*, an ideological paradigm that still appears to govern the Hollywood creation of the trustworthy black man. Each narrative genealogy of race and nation works in a structurally similar fashion: the imagining of the good black is dependent upon the rejection and removal of the alien black presence. Black saviors have to return to "Africa" or go to heaven. Though "Africa" as a literal reference point no longer functions in the same way that it did for Stowe, as a possible metaphoric and material place for disposing of an alien element that threatens to disrupt national unity, contemporary film directors do not have to explain to their audiences where black males are headed when they disappear from the screen. Hollywood can rely on the existence of the prison and the ghetto to function as equivalent spaces of exclusion in our contemporary political imagination.

As Glover walked out of a place in the heart of a Texas community, he walked into his first role as a police officer in *Witness* in 1985.[17] In this film Glover was still being cast in an ambiguous role. His character, McFee, is simultaneously inside of and outside of the law, a member of a police conspiracy to steal two and a half million dollars in drug money, and a cop who kills his fellow officers. Such ambiguity in relation to the law is resolved and ultimately transcended in *Lethal Weapon* and the series that followed.

A much more significant development in Glover's increasingly complex cinematic persona is his appearance, that same year, in Lawrence Kasdan's *Silverado*, a Western, in which he stars with Kevin Kline, Kevin Costner, and Glenn Scott.[18] At first *Silverado* looks as if it is going to merely reproduce elements from Glover's previous characterizations. Like Sally Field, Scott and Kline win Glover's loyalty after they do him a favor, saving him from arrest by a racist town sheriff played, most incongruously, by John Cleese. Glover's character later has occasion to accuse Kline of a lack of moral and ethical commitment when it appears that Kline's self-interest is steering him to support the wrong side in a battle between settlers and the evil cattle barons who have purchased the protection of the local, and extremely corrupt, law enforcement officials. Glover occupies the moral high ground and eventually persuades his white buddy to defend the settlers. A close friendship develops between them, a partnership that prefigures the relation between Kline and Glover in *Grand Canyon* and Mel Gibson and Glover in the *Lethal Weapon* series.

While Glover's Vietnam roles establish the historical source of the modern black male/white male partnership, *Silverado* brings out the homosocial and at times homoerotic nature of the relationship between white and black men—a homoeroticism that will eventually come to characterize much of the humor of the *Lethal Weapon* films. The "special" nature of the friendship between Kline and Glover in *Silverado* is established primarily through editing—the cross cutting of shot and counter-shot of glances or lingering looks, the creation of frequent eye-contact intended to suggest more than is spoken in words. The film is also homosocial and frequently phallocentric in many of its general techniques and effects. The mise-en-scene for the development of the relationship among all four men, as they travel across country, is a landscape replete with phallic imagery, a terrain that both evokes and sustains their commonality.

The cinematic chronology of Glover's fictional black masculinity advances another step toward patriarchal power in the role of Albert Johnson (Mister) in Steven Spielberg's film based on Alice Walker's novel, *The Color Purple* (1985).[19] Glover is a glowering, threatening patriarchal presence as a husband and father. Incapable of expressing emotion toward other men, not even for his own son and father, Mister represents the constant threat of violence against women. But this black patriarchal power and rage reign only over black women and younger black men, not over whites. However, the character Glover plays has to be capable of transformation as he ages alone, and has to persuade the audience that he atones. Clearly, Glover's experience with his previous film personifications, plus his talent, make this transformation convincing, and *The Color Purple* confirms that Glover can play both the brutal and the sensitive black man.[20]

Between 1987 and 1992, Danny Glover starred in a number of films which reproduced the ideological terms within which the utopian dimensions of Hollywood's contemporary interracial masculine romance are imagined and secured. The historical experience of Vietnam is evoked as the source of this romance—a partnership which establishes equality in the shared experience of war and defeat. In Glover's own film genealogy, his role as Captain Bartholomew Clark in *Bat 21* (1988), as Sergeant Roger Murtaugh in the *Lethal Weapon* series (1987, 1989, and 1992), and as Frank "Dookie" Camparelli in *Flight of the Intruder* (1990) provide substantial examples of the cinematic black and white masculine partnerships that transcend racialization.

Flight of the Intruder, in which Glover stars with Willem Dafoe and Brad Johnson, elaborates on the persona Glover plays in *Bat 21*.[21] As Captain of a U.S. Navy aircraft carrier off the coast of Vietnam in September 1972, Glover plays the part of an authoritarian but nurturing parental male toward the younger men in his charge. A strict but caring disciplinarian, Glover wins the respect and love of his subordinates. "Christ, all we've really got is each other," he teaches them. The armed forces are represented as an all-male substitute or equivalent for the family, a unit which excludes women. In this homosocial order race is not *the* important issue; the principal concern is with ways of bonding. For example, in *Flight* Frank Camparelli identifies himself, and is characterized by others, as a Mafia boss. The reference to the Mafia, con-firmed by his surname, evokes an alternative and familial structure of patriarchal allegiance, power, and control. This kind of homosocial partnership has become of increasing importance to male Hollywood film directors in developing an explicitly antifeminist male culture.

Richard Donner's *Lethal Weapon* series exemplifies this interracial male alliance against women.[22] Considered together, the three films document the development of a close and increasingly intimate partnership between an older black and a younger white male. But the origin of this phenomenon does not lie in the history of the movement to gain civil rights. It is the history of the desegregation of the United States armed forces and the "policing" of Southeast Asia that enables the relationship of equality between Martin Riggs and Roger Murtaugh. Men become buddies not in a movement for liberation but in a shared experience as oppressors, and their friendships are born outside the continental United States. What Riggs and Murtaugh share is the experience of Vietnam, which is the ground of their apparent equality and the basis for their mutual respect.

Lethal Weapon, the first in the series, forges Riggs and Murtaugh into an unbeatable fighting team as they defeat a rogue group of special forces mercenaries against a Los Angeles landscape that increasingly resembles Vietnam as the film progresses. Like Kasdan, Donner recreates Vietnam within Los Angeles. "We're gonna get bloody on this one, Roger. . . . You'll just have to trust me," Riggs declares. Both Murtaugh and Riggs are captured and tortured and have to learn that all they can trust, all they can rely on is each other. In the closing moment of the film, the rain-soaked muddy fields of Vietnam are explicitly evoked as Riggs is involved in hand to hand combat on Murtaugh's front lawn, which is being drenched by a burst hydrant.[23]

In *Lethal Weapon 2*, the national significance of their partnership is established in a battle to save the nation from a drug cartel run by South African diplomats. Riggs and Murtaugh's partnership and friendship also advance in this film. When the diplomats call Riggs a "Kaffir-lover," his antiracist credentials are secured. In *Lethal Weapon 3*, Los

Angeles and Vietnam are again fused in the landscape as the two heroes wage war against a home-grown enemy who has declared war on the entire L.A.P.D., a police force which at this stage of the series is on the front line of a battle to save the nation.

The Murtaugh-Riggs partnership does not so much exclude women as relegate them to their proper sphere. In the first *Lethal Weapon*, when each man is still rather wary of the other, they share a joke about Trish Murtaugh's (Darlene Love) cooking. In the sequel Riggs and Murtaugh virtually share in the fruits of Trish's domestic labor. "Where does Trish keep my laundry, man?" queries Riggs, and they both agree that if only the bad guys had planted their bomb in Trish's stove rather than in the Murtaughs' bathroom, "they could have ended a lot of needless suffering right there."

The relationship between Riggs and Murtaugh has an explicitly homoerotic dimension which seems both to attract and repel Richard Donner. The film constantly flirts with homoeroticism and parodies it in a homophobic manner. In the first film, "What are you, a fag?" shouts Riggs, in response to Murtaugh's jumping on top of him to try to extinguish the flames that engulf his body. *Lethal Weapon 2* has a series of running jokes that spin out of a scene in which Murtaugh is trapped, sitting on a toilet rigged to explode if he should stand up. In *Lethal Weapon 3* the homoeroticism is somewhat more mature and less directly inspired by anal humor. But at the same time Donner is clearly fascinated by the representation of homosexual attraction. As *Lethal Weapon 2* ends, Riggs is in Murtaugh's arms, possibly fatally injured. Their verbal exchange condenses the conflicted and contradictory aura of homoeroticism. "You're not dead until I tell you," insists Murtaugh, "now breathe!" Riggs's response is, "Did anyone ever tell you, you really are a beautiful man? Give us a kiss before they come." "Where did that bullet hit you anyway?" Murtaugh wants to know. The ambiguity of this exchange is left unresolved and perhaps even heightened by Donner's choice of closing music, George Harrison's "Cheer Down." As the credits roll Harrison sings,

There's no tears to be shed
Gonna love you instead
I want you around
Cheer down.[24]

In *Grand Canyon*, however, Kasdan deliberately distances his male characters from the homoeroticism that permeates the *Lethal Weapon* series. When the noise of the helicopter which opens the film fades, a basketball net appears, surrounded by black hands reaching upward. In a black-and-white opening sequence on an urban basketball court, the camera wanders over the bodies of the black players, torsos, legs, hands, and feet. There is a clear visual analogy with the second half of the credit sequence, which takes place in the Forum and is filmed in color. However, the force of the analogy is not established in the black-white commonality of the basketball court, a site which is reserved for the safe portrayal of interracial intimacy among men; rather, the analogy works through the gaze of the camera over black male bodies in the first sequence and the sexually predatory gaze of Mack across the court at the women who walk by. In this part of the credit sequence again the camera lingers over parts of bodies, particularly the torsos and bouncing breasts of the women as they walk in rhythm to the music.

Certainly Mack's blatant stare of sexual desire at these passing female bodies is intended to emphasize his heterosexuality and to prevent any misinterpretation of his later feelings for Simon. But these opening sequences and the confrontation scene that follows do establish the cultural spaces the film designates as safe. Safe spaces are cultural sites in which whites can be in close proximity to, intimate with, and gaze at black bodies. The two opening sequences, the neighborhood basketball court and the Forum game, prefigure the nature of the close relationship that develops between Simon and Mack; a friendship that comes to a cinematic climax when they play basketball with each other in Mack's driveway.

In *Lethal Weapon 3*, one particular scene highlights the relationship between Martin Riggs and Roger Murtaugh. This scene thoroughly dissects the terms and conditions of their friendship, attempting to cast it in the mythical dimensions of the relationship between Huck and Jim on their raft in Mark Twain's 1885 novel, *Adventures of Huckleberry Finn*.[25] Riggs and Murtaugh face a crisis as partners and as friends, a crisis as serious as that faced by Huck and Jim when they missed the entry into the Ohio river and sailed ever deeper into the slave states of the South. In Mark Twain's novel, this mistake clinched the historical terms and conditions of Jim's existence and his dependence on Huck Finn: as a black male, in order to survive he had to "belong" to someone.

In *Lethal Weapon 3*, in a similar fashion, Donner reworks the contemporary terms and conditions of the relationship between his white and black male protagonists. The crisis has been precipitated by two events: Murtaugh is agonizing over the fact that in an armed confrontation he shot and killed a fifteen-year old young black male whom he discovered to be his son's best friend; Riggs is distraught because their partnership is about to be dissolved when Murtaugh retires from the force in just three days.

This long, eight-minute segment explores the complex and contradictory possibilities for expressing interracial male intimacy, and while the scene is, at times, intensely homoerotic, it also closes off, both visually and verbally, the possibility that this intimacy could encompass a homosexual relation. As Huck and Jim's navigational error determined the public nature of their relation to each other, so Donner opens this scene in a way that determines what follows.

Riggs goes to find Murtaugh, who is hiding out on his boat drinking whiskey. He finds Murtaugh drunk and apparently out of control. Murtaugh holds a gun to Riggs's head and, in clichéd terms, threatens to harm the best friend he ever had. Why would Murtaugh betray his friend, his "brother" who has clearly demonstrated his loyalty to him? The moment is fraught with the tension of Riggs's agony and the betrayal he feels at Murtaugh's imminent retirement. This tension creates and reproduces on the screen a contemporary political anxiety: that black America, having demanded and gained equality, has somehow betrayed the white and middle-class America that graciously acceded to these demands. The political effect is that when Riggs shouts at Murtaugh, "You selfish bastard," a large segment of white male America makes the same accusation.

The accusation of the betrayal of white America by an aggressive black America informs and shapes the work of a number of contemporary liberal political analysts. Andrew Hacker, in *Two Nations: Black and White, Separate, Hostile and Unequal*, addresses this anxiety and argues that the processes of equalization and nationalization imagined to be inherent in the social consensus to grant civil rights were, indeed, only imaginary. He concludes that such a consensus no longer exists and that America must be regarded as two separate nations confronting each other. Hacker situates his discussion of the liberal anxiety evident in this political crisis in the context of the black urban rebellions of the late 1960s.

> After those disturbances, race relations never returned to their former plane. Whites ceased to identify black protests with a civil rights movement led by students and ministers. Rather, they saw a resentful and rebellious multitude, intent on imposing its presence on the rest of society. Blacks were seen as trying to force themselves into places and positions where they were not wanted or for which they lacked the competence. As the 1970s started, so came a rise in crimes, all too many of them with black perpetrators. By that point, many white Americans felt they had been betrayed. Worsening relations between the races were seen as largely due to the behavior of blacks, who had abused the invitations to equal citizenship white America had been tendering.[26]

Hacker's belief that white Americans have lost all sympathy for black Americans shapes his political agenda.

Belief in this apparent lack of sympathy also influences Donner's decision to locate the source for his characters' mutual respect in Southeast Asia rather than in the history of the struggle for civil rights. Hacker attempts to regain this lost sympathy through an extraordinary performance of intellectual blackface. In a chapter called "Being Black in America," in which he imagines what it would be like to be black, he reveals an intense masculine anxiety about black male bodies.

Hacker is only one of many political critics who are busily constructing genealogies of race and nation that are centrally concerned with white male anxiety, particularly liberal anxiety, about relationships with black men. His argument that white men feel betrayed by actually or potentially rebellious black men is echoed in Thomas Edsall's very influential book, *Chain Reaction: The Impact of Race, Rights, and Taxes on American Politics*, in which such betrayal is used to explain the alienation of white Democratic [male] voters from the special-interest politics of racial injustice.[27] In the popular cultural imagination such anxiety is most frequently paired with the nightmarish landscape of urban crisis.

What *Grand Canyon*, the *Lethal Weapon* series, and a number of other contemporary Hollywood films have in common is their unspoken attempt to resolve and overcome a national, racialized crisis through an intimate interracial male partnership. What Danny Glover's cinematic career illustrates is a sequence of performances of black manhood which embodies all the ethical codes of white middle-class America. What Kasdan incorporates into *Grand Canyon* and Donner utilizes in the *Lethal Weapon* series is the national embodiment of the perfect black male: a sensitive black father and relentless seeker of justice. The Danny Glover persona has become the lethal weapon that is wielded by Hollywood directors to fight representations of black men that they define and create as dangerous. The cultural construction of the bad guy is a direct political response to the national bourgeois dilemma: how to distinguish the good from the bad black men.[28]

In *Grand Canyon* Kasdan grants Simon the moral authority to deny common humanity to the rebellious "gang" of five young men. This moral authority is acquired gradually and in a number of ways. First, Simon manages to extricate Mack and himself from the clutches of the young men without resorting to violence. He establishes who made the call for help and then continues to talk to Mack about the problem with the car as if the others weren't there. This behavior is quickly identified by the young men as a sign of disrespect. Next, Simon tries to persuade them that he is just doing his job. As the young men are unresponsive to the terms of the work ethic, Simon tries another tactic. He identifies the young man he supposes is the leader and takes him aside. He explains that he is responsible for the truck, Mack's car, and Mack himself and asks, as a favor, to be allowed to go on his way. This exchange is a very important moment because it establishes the ground upon which Simon's role as a mouthpiece for the philosophy of the film will be built. The young man asks: "Are you askin' me a favor as a sign of respect, or are you askin' me a favor 'cos I got the gun?" Simon pauses and then replies: "Man, the world ain't supposed to work like this, maybe you don't know that but this ain't the way it's supposed to be. I'm supposed to be able to do my job without asking you if I can. That dude is supposed to be able to wait with his car without you ripping him off. Everything is supposed to be different than what it is." The young man is clearly puzzled by this response and says, "So, what's your answer?" To which Simon replies, "You don't have the gun, we ain't having this conversation," which gets the response, "That's what I thought, no gun, no respect, that's why I always carry the gun."

Having made the point that Simon can voice the moral codes and ethics of the middle class and be streetwise at the same time, the Simon character is also used to dehumanize the young men. In a conversation with Mack that takes place back at the service station while waiting for the car to be fixed, Simon adopts a folksy persona, a persona from which many Americans seem to draw comfort, and compares the young men to predatory sharks. Simon explains to Mack that what happened to him was a matter of chance, that "one day, just one particular day you bump into the big shark." "Now the big shark don't hate you, he has no feelings for you at all, you look like food to him. . . . Those boys back there, they got nothing to lose. If you just happen to be swimming along and bump into them, well . . . It might not be worth worrying about; it's like being in a plane crash." Once he has dismissed these "boys" from the realm of humanity, they can be conveniently forgotten. They do not appear again in the film and presumably disappear into jail, say, or become urban homicide statistics. For do we really care or even think about what happens to sharks as long as they aren't preying upon us? What inspires fear has been identified, given a body, but no name. The young black men presented as "gang" have served their purpose. This use of Glover to annihilate an aggressive black male force is even more explicit in *Predator 2*, in which the streets of Los Angeles have become "a slaughterhouse." Pitted against Jamaican drug lords, King Willie and his Voodoo posse, Glover also expels an extraterrestrial predator with long locks.

But in addition to playing a crucial role in the expulsion of an alien black presence in films like *Grand Canyon*, the *Lethal Weapon* series, *Dead Man Out* (1989), and more recent films like *The Saint of Fort Washington* (1993), Glover has performed another important role: that of father confessor and psychological counsellor to white men. In these films he acts as a sympathetic ear and a wise man, fostering the psychological healing of white men damaged by the stresses of postmodern life. Glover has become identified as the one who manages to persuade white men to recognize, understand, and express the truth about themselves to themselves. In his person Hollywood, in addition to producing the black male as an outcast who threatens to undermine the very foundations of America, adopts the black man as a sympathetic cypher, a means for white men to find meaning within themselves and discover the true meaning of their existence. On the one hand, these meanings are established for the audience of these films but, on the other, they reflect the values of the producers and directors. In their minds and films reside myriad references, meanings, and relationships that can be endlessly drawn upon and recycled. Glover has come to occupy a particularly important position as a teller of stories that modern America needs to hear, an urban folk figure still in touch with the most important social values and ethics which a postmodern society is in danger of forgetting.

These intimate black and white male partnerships, which exclude women, project the black masculinity imagined by white male liberals in quest of perfect partners. Together and alone, these race men of Hollywood dreams promise to annihilate what ails this nation and resolve our contemporary crisis of race, of nation, and of manhood. If we are to expose the exploitative and oppressive nature of such dream-work, we must reclaim the political commitment of Paul Robeson who challenged cultural workers, artists, and intellectuals to take a stand. Are we going to elect for freedom or slavery? Are we going to preserve this "threadbare" masculinity? Or are we going to burn it?

NOTES

Introduction

1. St. Clair Drake and Horace Cayton, *Black Metropolis: A Study of Life in a Northern City* (New York: Harcourt Brace, 1945), pp. 390–392.

2. Drake and Cayton, *Black Metropolis*, p. 394.

3. It is interesting to note that in the white press the term "Race Man" appears in quotation marks, whereas in the black press it doesn't.

4. Alfred A. Moss, *The American Negro Academy: Voice of the Talented Tenth* (Baton Rouge: Louisiana State University Press, 1981), pp. 35, 49.

5. In 1898 Maritcha B. Lyons was asked to present a paper. It was read by E. D. Barrier, as Lyons could not attend. In 1908, at a panel discussion on education, a woman was asked her opinion. These are the only two occasions in which women were asked to participate. See Moss, *The American Negro Academy*, pp. 78, 134.

6. Wilson Jeremiah Moses (1989), *Alexander Crummell: A Study of Civilization and Discontent* (rpt. Amherst: University of Massachusetts Press, 1992), p. 10.

7. See Cornel West, *Race Matters* (Boston: Beacon Press, 1993), p. 40.

8. Philip Brian Harper, *Are We Not Men? Masculine Anxiety and the Problem of African American Identity* (New York: Oxford University Press, 1996), p. x.

1. The Souls of Black Men

1. See Julius Lester, ed., *The Seventh Son: The Thought and Writings of W. E. B. Du Bois* (New York: Vintage, 1971), p. 24. Cornel West characterizes the sacrificial nature of Du Bois's intellectual project as a "Victorian strategy." See Henry Louis Gates, Jr. and Cornel West, *The Future of the Race* (New York: Knopf, 1996), p. 64.

2. W. E. B. Du Bois (1903), *The Souls of Black Folk* (rpt. New York: New

American Library, 1982). Page numbers to this edition will hereafter be cited in parenthesis in the body of the text.

3. Gates and West, *Future of the Race*, p. 65.

4. Gates and West, *Future of the Race*, pp. 58–79.

5. The use of the phrase "real intellectual work" points to what I believe is the relegation of feminist analysis to the realm of domestic intellectual labor. Male intellectuals do the real work of intellectual labor, whereas feminist or gender analysis applies only to the separate sphere of women.

6. West severely criticizes Du Bois's model of the "Talented Tenth" for being elitist; see Gates and West, *The Future of the Race*, pp. 65–67. West is equally uninterested in and dismissive of feminist work. See, for example, p. 185 n.20, on Ida B. Wells, which ignores all scholarship on Wells by women. One can only assume that West does not read it.

7. W. E. B. Du Bois (1904), "The Development of a People," rpt. in David W. Blight and Robert Gooding-Williams, *The Souls of Black Folk* (Boston: Bedford Books, 1997), pp. 238–254.

8. I am, of course, rather freely but I hope not disrespectfully, both adopting and revising the term "structures of feeling" from Raymond Williams. While Williams applied this term to the "culture of a period," I want to retain this sense of history but also to evoke the cultural meanings of a particular text as I apply it to my readings of the essays collected in *The Souls of Black Folk*. Though I deviate slightly from Williams in my use of his insights, I am following the spirit and method of the conceptual framework, which he describes as follows: "The analysis of culture is the attempt to discover the nature of the organization which is the complex of these relationships. Analysis of particular works or institutions is, in this context, analysis of their essential kind of organization, the relationships which works or institutions embody as parts of the organization as a whole. A keyword, in such analysis, is pattern: it is with the discovery of patterns of a characteristic kind that any useful cultural analysis begins, and it is with the relationships between these patterns, which sometimes reveal unexpected identities and correspondences in hitherto separately considered activities, sometimes again reveal discontinuities of an unexpected kind, that general cultural analysis is concerned." Raymond Williams (1961), *The Long Revolution* (rpt. London: Pelican Books, 1965), pp. 63–66.

9. Wesley Brown in Louis Massiah, dir., *W. E. B. Du Bois: A Biography in Four Voices* (San Francisco: California Newsreel, 1995), part 1.

10. It is, however, the case that in his private life, as a father and as a husband, Du Bois was a consummate patriarch, but that is not the subject of my concern in this chapter. For further consideration of the contradictions that existed between Du Bois's public politics and his private life, contradictions that are not

uncommon in the lives of men who publicly support feminist causes, see David Levering Lewis, *W. E. B. Du Bois: Biography of a Race, 1868–1919* (New York: Henry Holt, 1993).

11. Gates and West, *Future of the Race*, p. 55.

12. See also William Andrews, *Critical Essays on W. E. B. Du Bois* (Boston: G. K. Hall, 1985), for a selection of early reviews of the book.

13. James Weldon Johnson, *The Autobiography of An Ex-Colored Man* (1912) (rpt. New York: Hill and Wang, 1960), pp. 168–169. Johnson also evokes Du Bois's metaphor of the veil in his Preface: "In these pages it is as though a veil had been drawn aside: the reader is given a view of the inner life of the Negro in America, is initiated into the freemasonry, as it were, of the race" (p. xii). Johnson, like Du Bois, privileges discourses of masculinity and assumes that these will reveal the inner life of the race as a whole. See Robert B. Stepto, *From Behind the Veil: A Study of Afro-American Narrative* (Urbana: University of Illinois Press, 1979), pp. 111–127, for a detailed explication of Johnson's use of *The Souls of Black Folk*. See also Valerie Smith, *Self-Discovery and Authority in Afro-American Narrative* (Cambridge: Harvard University Press, 1987), pp. 56–58.

14. James Weldon Johnson, *Along This Way: The Autobiography of James Weldon Johnson* (1933) (rpt. New York: Viking Penguin, 1990), p. 203.

15. The phrase "imagined community" is, of course, taken from Benedict Anderson, *Imagined Communities: Reflections on the Origins and Spread of Nationalism* (London: Verso, 1983), see p. 62. For a description of genealogies and their relation to "homogenous empty time," see pp. 68–69.

16. In the context of discussing religious pilgrimages, Benedict Anderson argues that "a vast horde of illiterate vernacular-speakers provided the dense, physical reality of the ceremonial passage; while a small segment of literal bilingual adepts drawn from each vernacular community performed the unifying rites, interpreting to their respective followings the meaning of their collective motion." Anderson, *Imagined Communities*, p. 56. I see *The Souls of Black Folk* as performing a similar interpretive function of bringing a people into existence, and regard the intellectual act of producing the text as analogous to "performing the unifying rites."

17. See Andrews, *Critical Essays*, for reprints of these essays: Houston A. Baker, Jr. (1972), "The Black Man of Culture: W. E. B. Du Bois and *The Souls of Black Folk*," pp. 129–138; Darwin T. Turner (1974), "W. E. B. Du Bois and the Theory of a Black Aesthetic," pp. 73–91; and Wilson J. Moses (1975), "The Poetics of Ethiopianism: W. E. B. Du Bois and Literary Black Nationalism," pp. 92–105.

18. Arnold Rampersad, *The Art and Imagination of W. E. B. Du Bois* (Cambridge: Harvard University Press, 1976), pp. 88–89.

19. Stepto, *From Behind the Veil*, p. 99.

20. Indeed, I find the text very useful when I address the inherently interdisciplinary nature of work in African American Studies and American Studies, and as an example of the critical potential of African American cultural studies. However, it is also important to note that other works by Du Bois have not acquired such status and are not always in print. To state the obvious, there is a very real material relation between the process of the academic canonization of a text and the politics of the publishing industry.

21. W. E. B. Du Bois has been a consistent presence in the work of Cornel West as the figure of an ideal or representative African American intellectual. See, for example, *Prophesy Deliverance! An Afro-American Revolutionary Christianity* (Philadelphia: Westminster Press, 1982); *Prophetic Fragments* (Grand Rapids, MI.: Africa World Press, 1988); *The American Evasion of Philosophy: A Genealogy of Pragmatism* (Madison: University of Wisconsin Press, 1989); *Race Matters* (Boston: Beacon Press, 1993); and *Keeping the Faith: Philosophy and Race in America* (New York: Routledge, 1993).

22. Gates and West, *Future of the Race*, p. 55.

23. West, *American Evasion of Philosophy*, p. 138.

24. West, *American Evasion of Philosophy*, p. 5. Later, West describes his position as follows: "I began this work as an exercise in critical self-inventory, as a historical, social and existential situating of my own work as an intellectual, activist and human being. I wanted to make clear to myself my own contradictions and tensions, faults and foibles as one shaped by, in part, the tradition of American pragmatism" (p. 7).

25. West, *Keeping the Faith*, pp. 27, 82–83, 23.

26. West, *Race Matters*, p. 46.

27. See Anderson, *Imagined Communities*, p. 65. "Liberalism and the Enlightenment clearly had a powerful impact, above all in providing an arsenal of ideological criticisms of imperial and *ancien régimes*. What I am proposing is that neither economic interest, Liberalism, nor Enlightenment could, or did, create *in themselves* the *kind* or shape, of imagined community to be defended from these regime's depredations; to put it another way, none provided the framework of a new consciousness—the scarcely-seen periphery of its admiration or disgust. In accomplishing *this* specific task, pilgrim creole functionaries and provincial creole printmen played the decisive role."

28. The theoretical framework for my thinking about the narrative shape of genealogies is influenced by the work of Etienne Balibar and Immanuel Wallerstein, *Race, Nation, Class: Ambiguous Identities* (London: Verso, 1991).

29. See, for example, the analysis of Stepto, *From Behind the Veil*, pp. 3–31 and 67–72.

30. Mark Twain (1885), *Adventures of Huckleberry Finn* (rpt. New York: Library of America, 1982), pp. 704–716, 784.

31. Stepto, *From Behind the Veil*, p. 66.

32. For details of previous publication see Blight and Gooding-Williams, *Souls*, p. viii.

33. Cornel West shares this intellectual and political motivation with Du Bois: "I have written this text convinced that a thorough re-examination of American pragmatism, stripping it of its myths, caricatures, and stereotypes and viewing it as a component of a new and novel form of indigenous thought and action, may be a first step toward fundamental change and transformation in America and the world." *The American Evasion of Philosophy*, p. 8.

34. ". . . we have seen that the very conception of the newspaper implies the refraction of even 'world-events' into a specific imagined world of vernacular readers; and also how important to that imagined community is an idea of steady, solid simultaneity through time." Anderson, *Imagined Communities*, p. 63.

35. "How shall man measure Progress there where the dark-faced Josie lies? How many heartfuls of sorrow shall balance a bushel of wheat? How hard a thing in life to be lowly, and yet how human and real!" Du Bois, *Souls of Black Folk*, p. 108.

36. It is interesting that Du Bois himself recognizes the temptations of sensuality. "Golden apples are beautiful—I remember the lawless days of boyhood, when orchards in crimson and gold tempted me over fence and field" (p. 112). One can only wonder if writing the essay caused him to reflect upon his sexual relationship with Josie's mother. See n.37.

37. Du Bois clearly had somewhat ambivalent and complex attitudes toward female sexuality. In his autobiography he claims that when he taught in Tennessee he was "literally raped by the unhappy wife who was my landlady." David Levering Lewis states that this "unhappy wife" was Josie's mother. The claim of rape seeks to establish Du Bois's (male) innocence in the face of a predatory (female) sexuality. Du Bois appears to have considered female sexuality in binary terms as a conceptual dilemma. Whenever "I tried to solve the contradiction of virginity and motherhood I was inevitably faced with the other contradiction of prostitution and adultery." It is interesting to reflect upon what Du Bois calls here, "a contradiction," in light of the binary gendered structures of thought and feeling in *Souls*. See W. E. B. Du Bois, *The Autobiography of W. E. B. Du Bois*

(New York: International Publishers, 1968), p. 280; and David Levering Lewis, *W. E. B. Du Bois: Biography of a Race: 1868–1919* (New York: Henry Holt, 1993), pp. 68–72.

As Claudia Tate has reminded me, Du Bois does later use a female figure for social transformation as the character of Zora in *The Golden Fleece*.

38. West, *Race Matters*, p. 40. As West's clothing duplicates Du Bois's, one assumes that he may be adopting the values that Du Bois imagined went along with the way he dressed. Indeed, the photograph on the cover of *Race Matters* would seem to confirm this analogy. However, one must take issue with West's cavalier dismissal of how other black intellectuals dress, and with the intellectual and political implications he draws from it.

39. David Levering Lewis considers that the "elegiac prose of 'The Passing of the First-Born' verges on bathos today." I have called it "passionate" but we both seem to agree that the focus of the tragedy is Du Bois himself. However, because I see such continuity between this essay and the other essays in *The Souls of Black Folk*, I would disagree with Levering Lewis's opinion that the essay is merely an "apostrophe" in the book. See Levering Lewis, *W. E. B. Du Bois*, p. 227.

40. Gates and West, *Future of the Race*, pp. 48–49.

41. Gates and West, *Future of the Race*, pp. 27–29.

42. As Etienne Balibar has described the particular conditions of racism in the modern world: "societies in which racism develops are at the same time supposed to be 'egalitarian' societies, in other words, societies which (officially) disregard status differences between individuals, this sociological thesis . . . cannot be abstracted from the national environment itself . . . it is not the modern state which is 'egalitarian' but the modern (nationalist) nation-state, this equality having as its internal and external limits the national community and, as its essential content, the acts which signify it directly (particularly universal suffrage and political 'citizenship'). It is, first and foremost, an equality in respect of nationality." See Balibar and Wallerstein, *Race, Nation, Class*, pp. 49–50. Benedict Anderson has also pointed out the force of these contradictions: the nation "is imagined as a community, because, regardless of the actual inequality and exploitation that may prevail in each, the nation is always conceived as a deep, horizontal comradeship." Anderson, *Imagined Communities*, p. 16.

43. Balibar and Wallerstein, *Race, Nation, Class*, p. 50. As Balibar describes this process, "the connection between nationalism and racism is neither a matter of perversion (for there is no 'pure' essence of nationalism) nor a question of formal similarity, but a question of historical articulation."

44. See also Du Bois's essay, "The Conservation of the Races," and the

discussion of it by Blight and Gooding-Williams in their Introductory essay to *The Souls of Black Folk*, p. 9.

45. Anderson, *Imagined Communities*, p. 53: "The success of the Thirteen Colonies' revolt at the end of the 1770s, and the onset of the French Revolution at the end of the 1780s, did not fail to exert a powerful influence. Nothing confirms this 'cultural revolution' more than the pervasive *republicanism* of the newly-independent communities. Nowhere was any serious attempt made to recreate the dynastic principle in the Americas, except in Brazil. . . ."

46. I refer to the trappings and hierarchy of Empire that were reproduced in U.N.I.A. parades and costumes and in the titles given to U.N.I.A. officials.

47. It would be an interesting and fruitful project to trace the use of gender as a term of mediation between the concept of race and the evocation of the premodern dynastic order in the work of Marcus Garvey and in the U.N.I.A.

48. Gates's experience as described in his essay "The Parable of the Talents" bears an uncanny similarity to Du Bois's account of his educational success and the failures of the other boys. At the end of the section which includes the passage of loss and mourning quoted above, Gates concludes: "But I was fortunate; I loved the place [Yale]. I loved the library and the seminars, I loved talking with the professors; I loved 'peeping the hole card' in people's assumptions and turning their logic back upon themselves. I had more chip than shoulder, and through it all I demanded of every person with whom I chanced to interact that they earn the right to learn my name. . . . Only sometimes do I feel guilty that I was among the lucky ones, and only sometimes do I ask myself why." For both Gates and Du Bois, their success in negotiating their way as intellectuals lies in the complexity of their formation as particular types of men. Gates and West, *Future of the Race*, pp. 51–52.

49. David Levering Lewis directs our attention to how very many different autobiographical versions of the moment of Du Bois's discovery of the significance of race there are in his writings. However, he also seems to agree that Du Bois's awareness of race is consistently gendered. "Whatever the personal dynamics of racial self-discovery were, by his thirteenth birthday Willie came to have an informed idea of what being a black male meant even in the relatively tolerant New England." See Levering Lewis, *W. E. B. Du Bois*, pp. 33–34.

50. West, *Race Matters*, pp. 88–89.

51. It is worth noting that Cornel West too treats himself as an exception among other black men in his analysis of the politics of contemporary black male sexuality, and that he consciously styles his body to be a conspicuous sign of that distinction. Of course, using the body to display masculine distinction as "race leader" is not limited to Du Bois and Cornel West. Marcus Garvey, for

example, comes immediately to mind. All three have used their bodies to articulate masculine exceptionalism in particularly interesting ways.

52. David Levering Lewis speculates how possibly "evasive, ambivalent and wretched Du Bois's feelings for his mother might have been as she became an 'albatross' to him." Levering Lewis, *W. E. B. Du Bois*, p. 52.

53. I am concentrating upon the function of intellectuals here and following a Gramscian definition of intellectual practices, as follows: "Can one find a unitary criterion to characterise equally all the diverse and disparate activities of intellectuals and to distinguish these at the same time and in an essential way from the activities of other social groupings? The most widespread error of method seems to me that of having looked for this criterion of distinction in the intrinsic nature of intellectual activities, rather than in the ensemble of the system of relations in which these activities (and therefore the intellectual groups who personify them) have their place within the general complex of social relations. . . . All men are intellectuals . . . but not all men have in society the function of intellectuals. When one distinguishes between intellectuals and non-intellectuals, one is referring in reality only to the immediate social function of the professional category of the intellectuals." Antonio Gramsci, *Selections from the Prison Notebooks* (London: Lawrence and Wishart, 1971), pp. 8, 9.

54. The use of "incorporation" refers to the thesis Alan Trachtenberg developed in his book, *The Incorporation of America: Culture and Society in the Gilded Age* (New York: Hill and Wang, 1982).

55. Eric Hobsbawm, as quoted in Anderson, *Imagined Communities*, p. 69.

2. The Body and Soul of Modernism

1. Absolutely indispensable is the collection of essays in two volumes by William Rubin, ed., *Primitivism in 20th Century Art: Affinity of the Tribal and the Modern* (New York: The Museum of Modern Art, 1984). See also James Clifford, "Negrophilia," in Denis Hollier, ed., *A History of New French Literature* (Cambridge, MA.: Harvard University Press, 1989), pp. 901–907; Wyndham Lewis, *Paleface: The Philosophy of the Melting Pot* (London: Chatto and Windus, 1929); and Marianna Torgovnick, *Gone Primitive: Savage Intellects, Modern Lives* (Chicago: University of Chicago Press, 1990).

2. James Weldon Johnson, *Along This Way: The Autobiography of James Weldon Johnson* (1933) (rpt. New York: Penguin, 1990), pp. 317–318.

3. W. E. B. Du Bois, *The Souls of Black Folk* (1903) (rpt. New York: New American Library, 1969), p. xi.

4. I do not wish to suggest that black women and children were not lynched;

they were. My concentration on black male bodies is not intended to neglect this.

5. As always I am deeply indebted to the work and comradeship of Paul Gilroy.

6. Gail Bederman, *Manliness and Civilization: A Cultural History of Gender and Race in the United States, 1880–1917* (Chicago: University of Chicago Press, 1995).

7. Johnson, *Along this Way*, p. 412.

8. Elizabeth Shepley Sergeant, "The Man with His Home in a Rock: Paul Robeson," *New Republic*, March 3, 1926: 40–44.

9. Sergeant, "The Man with His Home in a Rock," p. 40.

10. See entry "Muray, Nickolas" in the *International Center of Photography Encyclopedia of Photography* (New York: Crown Publishers, 1984), pp. 348–349; the Introduction by Marianne Fulton Margolis to Nickolas Muray, *Muray's Celebrity Portraits of the Twenties and Thirties: 135 Photographs by Nickolas Muray* (New York: Dover Publications, and International Museum of Photography at George Eastman House, 1978); and "Biographical Material 1931–1964," and Paul Gallico, "Memento Muray," introduction to *The Revealing Eye*, undated typescript, *Nickolas Muray Papers*, Archives of American Art, Smithsonian Institution, Film 4392, Reels One and Two.

11. Nickolas Muray and Paul Gallico, *The Revealing Eye: Personalities of the 1920's in photographs by Nickolas Muray and words by Paul Gallico* (New York: Athenaeum, 1967).

12. "Autobiographical Notes," *Nickolas Muray Papers*, Reel One, pp. 2, 5.

13. See the portrait of Muray taken by Edward Steichen in the Introduction to Muray, *Celebrity Portraits*.

14. Muray, "Autobiographical Notes," p. 6.

15. Muray, "Autobiographical Notes," p. 15.

16. Peter Weiermair, *The Hidden Image: Photographs of the Male Nude in the Nineteenth and Twentieth Centuries* (Cambridge, MA.: MIT Press, 1988), p. 13. Though I disagree with Richard Dyer's reading of Muray's photographs of Robeson, I find his interpretation very provocative and interesting. Richard Dyer, *Heavenly Bodies: Film Stars and Society* (New York: St Martin's Press, 1986), pp. 120–124.

17. Weiermair, *The Hidden Image*, p. 13. He continues by describing the "Cult of the Body": "After World War I, the male nude was seen in a different light. This was due to several factors: modern sport, the Olympic Games, the back-to-nature movement, and the beginnings of modern nudism. The healthy, athletic look, a revival of the Greek ideal of a sane mind in a healthy body had always been beyond suspicion of eroticism. . . . Homosexual pinup magazines

emerged from the early publications of physical training and Akademien-like journals. . . . Such contemporary photographers as Robert Mapplethorpe and Bruce Weber cite these pictures, which still demonstrate the 'alibi of camouflage' " (p. 15).

18. Allen Ellenzweig, *The Homoerotic Photograph: Male Images from Durieu/Delacroix to Mapplethorpe* (New York: Columbia University Press, 1992), p. 15.

19. Muray and Gallico, *The Revealing Eye*, p. 239; Muray, *Muray's Celebrity Portraits*, p. 106.

20. The same effect can be found in the work of Robert Mapplethorpe, *The Black Book* (New York: St. Martin's Press, 1986).

21. See Estelle Jussim, *Slave to Beauty: The Eccentric Life and Controversial Career of F. Holland Day—Photographer, Publisher, Aesthete* (Boston: David R. Godine, 1981); Verna Posever Curtis and Jane Van Nimmen, *F. Holland Day: Selected Texts and Bibliography* (Oxford, England: CLIO Press, 1995); and Christian A. Peterson, *Alfred Steiglitz's Camera Notes* (New York: W. W. Norton, 1993).

22. Muray, "Autobiographical Notes," p. 10.

23. Ellenzweig, *The Homoerotic Photograph*, p. 2.

24. I agree with Ellenzweig when he insists that not only homosexuals create homoerotic art and that not only homosexuals have homoerotic feelings. He continues: "If the erotic base, or erotic possibility, of the male response to images of women is accepted without question, no such parallel 'automatic' response is built into our viewing of images of men." See Ellenzweig, *The Homoerotic Photograph*, pp. 2, 3. In my opinion it is important to distinguish between homoeroticism, which exists across the cultural spectrum, and homosexuality, which may be expressed in many cultural forms in a myriad of ways.

25. This is also true of F. Holland Day's black male nudes. See the photographs reproduced in this chapter along with "African Chief" and "The Smoker," also featuring Alfred Tanneyhill, in Jussim, *Slave to Beauty*.

26. "Ethiopian Form (1923)" is reproduced in Graham Howe and G. Ray Hawkins, eds., *Paul Outerbridge Jr.: Photographs* (New York: Rizzoli, 1980), p. 55. A related photograph entitled "Sleepy Negro, 1924" is reproduced in Elaine Dines, ed., *Paul Outerbridge: A Singular Aesthetic: Photographs and Drawings, 1921–1941* (Laguna Beach, CA: Laguna Beach Museum of Art, 1981), p. 84. Both photographs appear to be from the same session despite the difference in dates.

27. For an interesting discussion, upon which I draw, see Michael Hatt, " 'Making a Man of Him': Masculinity and the Black Body in Mid-Nineteenth-Century American Sculpture," *Oxford Art Journal* 15, 1 (1992):21–35.

28. Dorothy Donnell, *The New Art of Camera Painting*, p. 72; *Nickolas Muray Papers*, Reel 2.

29. Paul Gallico, "Memento Muray," pp. 26–27.

30. Nickolas Muray, quoted in Marianne Fulton Margolis, Introduction, *Muray's Celebrity Portraits of the Twenties and Thirties*; Muray, "Autobiographical Notes," *Nickolas Muray Papers*, Reel 1, pp. 9–10.

31. Alan Trachtenberg, *Reading American Photographs: Images as History, Mathew Brady to Walker Evans* (New York: Hill and Wang, 1989), p. 9.

32. Fredric Jameson, *Fables of Agression: Wyndham Lewis, the Modernist as Fascist* (Berkeley: University of California Press, 1979), p. 2.

33. H.D. to George Plank, 3 March 1930, *George Plank Papers*, Correspondence, Beinecke Library, Box 3, Folder 44.

34. See Anne Friedberg, "*Approaching* BORDERLINE," in Michael King ed., *H.D. Woman and Poet* (Orono, Maine: The National Poetry Foundation, 1986), pp. 369–390.

35. Publicity release, *BORDERLINE*, Studio Cinaes, typescript dated 1/3/1931, p. 1, *Bryher Papers*, Beinecke Library, Box 168, folder 5633.

36. Publicity release, p. 2.

37. H.D., *Borderline: A Pool Film with Paul Robeson*, (London: Mercury Press, 1930), pp. 16, 19.

38. Kenneth Macpherson, "As Is," *Close Up*, VII, 5 (Nov. 1930):293–294.

39. H.D., *Borderline*, pp. 36–37.

40. Kenneth Macpherson, "A Negro Film Union—Why Not?" in Nancy Cunard, ed., *The Negro: An Anthology* (London: Wishart, 1934), p. 336. Emphasis original.

41. H.D., "Two Americans," in *The Unusual Star*, privately printed by Imprimerie Darantiere, Dijon, France (1934), pp. 93–94.

42. H.D., "Two Americans," p. 116.

43. Oscar Micheaux, *Body and Soul* (New York: Micheaux Pictures Corporation, 1925). In addition to Robeson, the film starred (in alphabetical order) Chester A. Alexander, Lawrence Chenault, Walter Cornick, Mercedes Gilbert, Marshall Rogers, and Julia Theresa Russell. For an interesting but differently inflected discussion of black masculinity in Micheaux's films, see Charlene Register, "Oscar Micheaux's Multifaceted Portrayals of the African-American Male: The *Good*, the *Bad*, and the *Ugly*," in Pat Kirkham and Janet Thumim, eds., *Me Jane: Masculinity, Movies and Women* (London: Lawrence and Wishart, 1995), pp. 166–183. For a history of *Body and Soul*, see Thomas Cripps, *Slow Fade to Black: The Negro in American Film, 1900–1942* (New York: Oxford University Press, 1977), pp. 191–193.

44. See "All Negro Religious Drama," 1923 D 31, 9:5 and "Negroes Play

Roseanne," 1924 Mr 11, 16:3, in *The New York Times Theater Reviews 1920–1970*, vol 1, 1920–1926.

45. See Martin Bauml Duberman, *Paul Robeson* (New York: Knopf, 1988), pp. 56–57. On the Lafayette Players from among whom Micheaux drew the casts of many of his films, see Sister M. Francesca Thompson, O.S.F., "The Lafayette Players, 1917–1932," in Errol Hill, ed., *The Theatre of Black Americans* (New York: Applause, 1987), pp. 211–230. For Robeson's performance in *Roseanne*, see Samuel R. Delany, "Atlantis, Model 1924," in *Atlantis: Three Tales* (Hanover, NH: University Press of New England, 1995), pp. 37–38.

46. I have not been able to locate a copy of the play and so cannot compare it with the screenplay of the film. However, the plots seem to be identical, with the exception of the alter-ego of the Reverend, which seems to have been an invention of Micheaux, and the very awkward revelation that the entire plot is in fact a dream. See plot summaries in Burns Mantle, *The Best Plays of 1923–1924* (Boston: Small, Maynard, 1924), pp. 379–380; "*Roseanne*," in Samuel L. Leiter, ed., *The Encyclopedia of the New York Stage, 1920–1930 N-Z* (Westport, CT: Greenwood Press, 1985), p. 776; and the reviews in the *New York Times*.

47. Walter White, *The Fire in the Flint* (1924) (rpt. Athens, Georgia: University of Georgia Press, 1996). Duberman, *Robeson*, pp. 72–73. In 1931, Walter White succeeded James Weldon Johnson to the position of Secretary of the N.A.A.C.P.

48. One of the more bizarre accounts of Robeson's career at Rutgers is Earl Schenck Miers, *Big Ben* (Philadelphia: Westminster Press, 1942). *Big Ben* is in the genre of college novels and was brought to my attention by Kathy Newman, to whom I am very grateful. Miers presents Robeson as an elemental force of nature on the football field: "Ben arose, shaking the mistiness from his eyes, wiping the grime from his mouth. He was grateful for that brief contact with the soil; a Negro understood the strength of the earth. He wasn't afraid to sink his hands into it, to feel its warm, comforting pressure against his body, for out of the earth came power and stamina, the nutrients of life itself. Ben felt stronger because of the grime on his face, the dirt in his mouth. . . ." (pp. 46–47).

49. White, *Fire in the Flint*, pp. 13, 44–46.

50. White, *Fire in the Flint*, pp. 17–18.

51. White, *Fire in the Flint*, p. 24.

52. White, *Fire in the Flint*, p. 26.

53. Proverb used as epigraph to the novel.

54. White, *Fire in the Flint*, p. 271. Emphasis original.

55. Eugene O'Neill, *All God's Chillun Got Wings*, in *O'Neill: Complete Plays, 1920–1931* (New York: Library of America, 1988), pp. 277–315.

56. Stage directions, O'Neill, *All God's Chillun*, p. 279.

57. O'Neill, *All God's Chillun*, p. 284.

58. O'Neill, *All God's Chillun*, pp. 292–293.

59. Sidney Mintz, *Caribbean Transformations* (Baltimore, Maryland: Johns Hopkins University Press, 1974), p. 278.

60. Eugene O'Neill, *The Emperor Jones*, in *O'Neill: Complete Plays, 1913–1920*, p. 1030.

61. O'Neill, *The Emperor Jones*, p. 1033.

62. *The Emperor Jones* (1933), directed by Dudley Murphy. Screenplay by DuBose Heyward. Gifford Cochran Productions.

63. T. R. Poston, "Robeson to Play King Christophe in British Production, He Reveals," *New York Amsterdam News*, October 5, 1935:1–2.

64. The script for a revised version of this play is available as "The Black Jacobins" in Anna Grimshaw, ed., *The C. L. R. James Reader* (Oxford: Blackwell, 1992), pp. 67–111. C. L. R. James, *The Black Jacobins* (1938) (rpt. London: Allison & Busby, 1980).

65. See Duberman, *Robeson*, p. 634, n.32.

66. Paul Robeson, quoted in "Robeson Calls for Aid to Negroes Defending Democracy in Spain," *The Negro Worker*, June 1937, in Philip S. Foner, ed., *Paul Robeson Speaks, Writings, Speeches, Interviews, 1918–1974* (London: Quartet Books, 1978), p. 118.

67. Robeson, "Why I Joined Labor Theatre," in Foner, ed., *Paul Robeson Speaks*, p. 119. See also "Paul Robeson Joins Labor Theatre," *Daily Worker*, November 4, 1937, p. 7.

68. Colin Chambers, *The Story of Unity Theatre* (New York: St Martin's Press, 1989), pp. 107, 110, 117 and 137. See also Ralph Samuel, Ewan MacColl, and Stuart Cosgrove, *Theatres of the Left 1880–1935: Workers' Theatre Movements in Britain and America* (London: Routledge & Kegan Paul, 1984).

69. See Chambers, *Unity Theatre*, p. 151, and Duberman, *Robeson*, pp. 192, 223.

70. Chambers, *Unity Theatre*, p. 156.

71. "Paul Robeson Speaks for His People and All Humanity," *Sunday Worker*, November 14, 1937, p. 11.

72. Paul Robeson, *Here I Stand* (Boston: Beacon Press, 1958).

3. Tuning the American Soul

1. W. E. B. Du Bois (1903), *The Souls of Black Folk* (rpt. New York: New American Library, 1969).

2. Eric Sundquist, *To Wake the Nations: Race in the Making of American Literature* (Cambridge: Harvard University Press, 1993), p. 493. Although

Sundquist also points out that the lyrics of the spirituals are not reproduced, our interpretations concerning this absence are very different.

3. See Sundquist, *To Wake the Nations*, pp. 531–532, and Lawrence Levine, *Black Culture and Black Consciousness: Afro-American Folk Thought from Slavery to Freedom* (New York: Oxford University Press, 1977).

4. Sundquist, *To Wake the Nations*, p. 533.

5. Sundquist states that "Du Bois had before him no less a task than the creation of a black national culture—or rather, not so much its creation as the proof of its existence." I would argue that the former is the more significant task for *The Souls of Black Folk*, which does not imply that black culture did not exist before the writing of this text, but that Du Bois actively constructs a black cultural form *as* a national form of culture. This is one of Du Bois's most original contributions to black intellectual thought, and it is a mistake to think that *The Souls of Black Folk* has merely to give evidence of its existence. See Sundquist, *To Wake the Nations*, pp. 470, 484.

6. Sundquist argues as follows: "The establishment of an African American cultural poetics had to demonstrate the continued presence in America of an African culture where speech and song more closely approached each other on the continuum of cultural sound, where the vocalized talk of drums and rhythmic instruments was paramount, and where *nommo*, the power of the word in its oral dimension, governed human interaction to a far greater degree than in the Western tradition. Du Bois sought not to erase the Western, European American tradition but to balance it through a black ethnography capable of establishing the lyrical code lying within African American culture." Sundquist, *To Wake the Nations*, p. 485.

7. Sundquist, *To Wake the Nations*, p. 483. It remains unclear exactly how the bardic function produces the theoretical document. Sundquist's assertion that *The Souls of Black Folk* is the *first* "truly theoretical document in African American culture" is, to say the least, a controversial statement that would need careful historical documentation which he fails to provide.

8. Sundquist, *To Wake the Nations*, p. 484.

9. Carl Van Vechten, "Paul Robeson and Lawrence Brown," in Bruce Kellner, ed., *"Keep A-Inchin' Along": Selected Writings of Carl Van Vechten about Black Arts and Letters* (Westport, Conn.: Greenwood Press, 1979), pp. 154–158.

10. Martin Bauml Duberman, *Paul Robeson* (New York: Knopf, 1988), p. 81.

11. Quoted in Michael Neal, Liner Notes to *Paul Robeson: The Power and the Glory* (New York: Columbia Records, 474337 AAD), p. 13.

12. Rose Henderson, "Paul Robeson, Negro Singer," *Southern Workman* (April 1932):166 [emphasis mine].

13. Brown had been an accompanist to Roland Hayes, in London. Carl Van

Vechten characterizes Brown as a race man. He tells a story about Brown at a concert of Ernest Bloch's settings of the 114th and 137th psalms, sung by Povla Frijsh. "He read the statement of the composer in the program notes: 'In my music I have tried to express the soul of the Jewish people as I feel it.' On that day, race pride was born in the young negro's breast." Carl Van Vechten, "Paul Robeson and Lawrence Brown," in Kellner, ed., *Keep A-Inchin' Along*, p. 155.

14. These original Victor recordings were collected on *Songs of My People*, RCA Red Seal LM 3292 LP (1972). They were also reissued in Britain and added to recordings made by Gramophone. They are included on *Paul Robeson: A Lonesome Road* (London: Academy Sound and Vision, 1984) CD AJA 5027. My comments about Robeson and Brown's performances are in response to the Victor recordings.

15. See Neal, *Power and the Glory*, pp. 12–13; Van Vechten, "Robeson and Brown," pp. 155–157; Duberman, *Robeson*, pp. 78–79.

16. Neal, *Power and the Glory*, p. 13.

17. Eileen Southern, *The Music of Black Americans: A History* (New York: W. W. Norton, 1983), p. 268.

18. Carl Van Vechten, "Folksongs of the American Negro," in Kellner, ed., *Keep A-Inching Along*, p. 38.

19. James Weldon Johnson and J. Rosamund Johnson, *The Books of American Negro Spirituals* (1925 and 1926) (rpt. New York: Da Capo Press, 1977), p. 29.

20. Van Vechten, "Paul Robeson and Lawrence Brown," in Kellner, ed., *Keep A-Inchin' Along*, p. 156.

21. Robeson posed for this statue over a period of two years. Work on it began in 1924. See Duberman, *Robeson*, pp. 68–69.

22. Antonio Salemmé, quoted in Duberman, *Robeson*, p. 69.

23. Duberman, *Robeson*, p. 69.

24. Eslande Goode Robeson and Avery Robinson quoted in Duberman, *Robeson*, p. 79.

25. Langston Hughes quoted in Duberman, *Robeson*, p. 98.

26. Henderson, "Robeson," p. 166.

27. Paul Robeson, "I Breathe Freely," in Philip S. Foner, ed., *Paul Robeson Speaks: Writings, Speeches, Interviews, 1918–1974* (New York: Quartet Books, 1978), p. 100. Originally published in *New Theatre*, 2, 7, (July 1935):5.

28. Van Vechten, "Robeson and Brown," p. 155.

29. Van Vechten, "Robeson and Brown," p. 157.

30. Van Vechten, "Robeson and Brown," p. 158.

31. For an account of this occasion, which was thought to have "made radio history," see Duberman, *Robeson*, pp. 236–237.

32. Duberman, *Robeson*, p. 240.

33. Michael Denning, *The Cultural Front: The Laboring of American Culture in the Twentieth Century* (New York: Verso, 1997), p. 9.

34. Paul Robeson, *Ballad for Americans: Carnegie Hall Concert, Vol. 2*, RCA Victor VSD-79193. This original recording was with the American People's Chorus.

35. This account relies heavily upon Charles Wolfe and Kip Lornell, *The Life and Legend of Leadbelly* (New York: Harper Collins, 1992), pp. 110–113.

36. Paul Robeson, "Go Down Moses," *Paul Robeson: The Power and the Glory*, Columbia 1991, CK 47337.

37. John Lomax, *The Adventures of a Ballad Hunter*, as quoted in Wolfe and Lornell, *Leadbelly*, p. 111.

38. Wolfe and Lornell, *Leadbelly*, p. 120.

39. This description is drawn from the introductory essay to John A. and Alan Lomax, *Negro Folk Songs as Sung by Lead Belly* (New York: Macmillan, 1936), pp. 3–64.

40. Lomax and Lomax, *Negro Folk Songs*, p. xi.

41. *New York Herald Tribune*, January 3, 1935. As quoted in Wolfe and Lornell, *Leadbelly*, pp. 139, 141–142.

42. Lomax and Lomax, *Negro Folk Songs*, pp. 29–30.

43. I am indebted to Benjamin Filene for telling me about this newsreel. See also his excellent article, "'Our Singing Country': John and Alan Lomax, Leadbelly and the Construction of an American Past," *American Quarterly* 43, 4 (December 1991):602–624.

44. For a complete history, see Raymond Fielding, *The March of Time, 1935–1951* (New York: Oxford University Press, 1978).

45. "Leadbelly Footage," *March of Time Newsreel*, February, 1935 (New York: Archive Films).

46. Filene, "'Our Singing Country'":610.

4. Body Lines and Color Lines

1. For an account of the narratives of the Haitian revolution during this period, see Michael Denning, *The Cultural Front: The Laboring of American Culture in the Twentieth Century* (New York: Verso, 1997), pp. 396–397.

2. See Hazel V. Carby, "Proletarian or Revolutionary Literature: C. L. R. James and the Politics of the Trinidadian Renaissance," *South Atlantic Quarterly*

87, 1 (Winter 1988):39–52. I draw freely upon, revise, and extend this essay in this chapter. See also Denning, *The Cultural Front*.

3. C. L. R. James, *The Life of Captain Cipriani: An Account of British Government in the West Indies* (Nelson, Eng.: Coulton, 1932). For a rather different interpretation of the trajectory of James's work during this period, see Richard Small, "The Making of an Intellectual, the Making of a Marxist," *Urgent Tasks*, 12 (Summer 1981):13–18.

4. C. L. R. James, *Minty Alley* (1936) (rpt. London: New Beacon Books, 1971); *The Black Jacobins: Toussaint L'Ouverture and the San Domingo Revolution* (1938) (rpt. London: Allison and Busby, 1980).

5. For example, the first chapter of *Captain Cipriani* is organized into the following sections: The People Concerned; The English at Home; The Colonial Englishman; The White Creole; and The Colored People. Chapter 5, "Captain Cipriani and the Legislative Council," is subdivided into The Officials, The Unofficial Members, The Elected Members, The Governor in the Chair, and I Beg to Congratulate the Government. Compare this to *The Black Jacobins*, which has chapters that also structure the narrative according to classes as actors in history. For example, "The Property," "The Owners," "Parliament and Property," "The San Domingo Masses Begin, and the Paris Masses Complete."

6. James, *Captain Cipriani*, p. 1.

7. James, *Captain Cipriani*, pp. 6–7.

8. James, *Captain Cipriani*, p. 103.

9. James, *Captain Cipriani*, p. 101.

10. James was living with Constantine at the time, in Nelson, Lancashire, and the book was published with Constantine's help.

11. See C. L. R. James, "What Is Art," in Anna Grimshaw, ed., *The C. L. R. James Reader* (Oxford: Blackwell, 1992), pp. 315–326.

12. C. L. R. James, "A Great West Indian Batsman: Headley's Remarkable Rise to Fame," *Manchester Guardian*, April 18, 1933, in James, *Cricket*, Anna Grimshaw, ed. (New York: Allison and Busby, 1986), p. 11.

13. C. L. R. James, "The Greatest of All Bowlers: An Impressionist Sketch of S. F. Barnes," *Manchester Guardian*, September 1, 1932, in James, *Cricket*, p. 7.

14. Sylvia Wynter, "In Quest of Matthew Bondsman: Some Cultural Notes on the Jamesian Journey," *Urgent Tasks* 12 (Summer 1981):66.

15. C. L. R. James, "West Indies Cricket," *The Cricketer*, 6 May-24 June 1933, in James, *Cricket*, p. 14.

16. C. L. R. James, *Beyond a Boundary* (1963) (rpt. London: Stanley Paul, 1980).

17. E. P. Thompson, "C. L. R. James at 80," *Urgent Tasks*, 12 (Summer 1981): back cover.

18. W. E. B. Du Bois, *The Souls of Black Folk* (1903) (rpt. New York: New American Library, 1982), p. xii.

19. James, *Beyond a Boundary*, p. 72.

20. James, *Beyond a Boundary*, pp. 55, 60, and 72.

21. James, *Beyond a Boundary*, p. 71.

22. C. L. R. James, "Chances of West Indies in First Test," *Port of Spain Gazette*, 15 June 1933, in James, *Cricket*, pp. 34–35. Emphasis mine.

23. See James, *The Black Jacobins*, p. 25–26. "Men make their own history, and the black Jacobins of San Domingo were to make history which would alter the fate of millions of men and shift the economic currents of three continents. But if they could seize the opportunity they could not create it. The slave-trade and slavery were woven tight into the economics of the eighteenth century. . . . From the very momentum of their own development, colonial planters, French and British bourgeois, were generating internal stresses and intensifying internal rivalries, moving blindly to explosions and conflicts which would shatter the basis of their dominance and create the possibility of emancipation."

24. What follows is adapted from Carby, "Proletarian or Revolutionary Literature."

25. James, *Beyond a Boundary*, p. 17.

26. See the letter from James to Constance Webb, April 1936, in Anna Grimshaw, ed., *Special Delivery: The Letters of C. L. R. James to Constance Webb 1939–1948* (Cambridge, MA: Blackwell, 1996) p. 44.

27. For further details on the publishing history of these journals see Carby, "Proletarian or Revolutionary Literature," pp. 41–42; and Reinhard W. Sander, ed., *From Trinidad: An Anthology of Early West Indian Writing* (New York: Africana Publishing Co., 1978); and *The Beacon* (Port of Spain, Trinidad), vols. 1–4, no. 1 Mar. 1931–Nov. 1939 (Millwood, NY: Kraus Reprint, 1977).

28. Carby, "Proletarian or Revolutionary Literature," pp. 41–47.

29. For a more detailed discussion of this device see Carby, "Proletarian or Revolutionary Literature," pp. 49–50.

30. Grant Farred, "The Maple Man: How Cricket Made a Postcolonial Intellectual," in Farred, ed., *Re-thinking C. L. R. James* (Oxford: Blackwell, 1996), pp. 165–186.

31. Farred, "The Maple Man," p. 166.

32. James, *Beyond a Boundary*, p. 55.

33. James, *Beyond a Boundary*, p. 56.

34. Farred, "The Maple Man," p. 166.

35. James, *Beyond a Boundary*, p. 59.

36. Farred, "The Maple Man," p. 167.
37. James, *Beyond a Boundary*, p. 59.
38. James, *Minty Alley*, p. 37.
39. James, *Minty Alley*, p. 154.
40. I am particularly thinking of the character of Benoit in *Minty Alley*.
41. Arna Bontemps, *Black Thunder: Gabriel's Revolt: Virginia, 1800* (1936) (rpt. Boston: Beacon Press, 1968), p. 84.
42. Bontemps, *Black Thunder*, p. 79.
43. Bontemps, *Black Thunder*, pp. 81, 80, and 106.
44. See Samuel Delany, *Tales of Nevèrÿon* (1979) (rpt. Hanover, NH: Wesleyan University Press, 1993) and *Neveryóna* (New York: Bantam, 1983).
45. Guy Endore, *Babouk* (1934) (rpt. New York: Monthly Review Press, 1991).
46. Karl Marx, *The Eighteenth Brumaire of Louis Bonaparte* (1852) (rpt. New York: International Publishers, 1963), p. 15.
47. James, *The Black Jacobins*, p. 265, emphasis mine.
48. See Stephen Howe, *Anticolonialism in British Politics: The Left and the End of Empire, 1918–1964* (Oxford: Clarendon Press, 1993), particularly chap. 3, "The War Years, 1936–1945"; and Robert A. Hill, "In England, 1932–1938," *Urgent Tasks* 12 (Summer 1981): 19–27.
49. James, *The Black Jacobins*, pp. xi, 227.
50. See Denning, *The Cultural Front*, pp. 9–13 and 395–397, for a discussion of the politics of antifascism, antiracism, and anti-imperialism in popular front culture and in the series of texts that utilized the Haitian revolution as example.
51. The quotation continues: "James is not negating the fine arts. He is taking them out of the box in which bourgeois critical canons, responding to a socio-ideological code rather than to a purely critical conceptual imperative, have confined them." Wynter, "In Quest of Matthew Bondsman," p. 63.
52. James, *The Black Jacobins*, pp. x–xi.
53. Hill, "In England," p. 27.
54. W. E. B. Du Bois's *Black Reconstruction* was extremely influential for James and his associates. See C. L. R. James, *A History of Pan African Revolt* (1938) (rpt. Washington D.C.: Drum and Spear Press, 1969), p. 34. In chap. 3, "The Civil War," James adopts Du Bois's thesis that a general strike of the black people of the southern states took place immediately after the Emancipation Proclamation.
55. James, *The Black Jacobins*, p. 20.
56. James, *The Black Jacobins*, pp. 24–25.

57. James, *The Black Jacobins*, p. 18.
58. James, *The Black Jacobins*, p. 21.

5. Playin' the Changes

1. Samuel R. Delany, *The Motion of Light in Water: Sex and Science Fiction Writing in the East Village, 1960–1965* (1988) (rpt. New York: Masquerade Books, 1993); Miles Davis with Quincy Troupe, *Miles: The Autobiography of Miles Davis* (New York: Simon & Schuster, 1989).

2. David H. Rosenthal, *Hard Bop: Jazz and Black Music 1955–1965* (New York: Oxford University Press, 1992), p. 51, asserts that Davis's quintet, along with the quintet of Horace Silver, "created the hip sound of urban America." Much of Delany's fiction is concerned with urban America. As he has stated, "Clearly the Nevèrÿon series is a model of late twentieth-century (mostly urban) America. The question is, of course: What kind of model is it? This is not the same question as: Is it accurate or is it inaccurate? Rather: What sort of relation does it bear to the thing modeled? Rich, eristic, and contestatory (as *well* as documentary), I hope." Samuel R. Delany, *Return to Nevèrÿon* (Hanover, NH: University Press of New England, 1994), p. 286.

3. Davis, *Miles*, p. 7.

4. Delany, *Motion of Light*, p. 4.

5. The loss of the father and the questions of authority embedded in father figures resonate throughout Delany's fiction. See, for example *Neveryóna*: "Yes, all of them were authorities for her. She did what they seemed to ask when they confronted her. When they were not there, she found herself still doing what they might want, as though all of them only stood for that obsessive, absent father who was with her always. Oh, he listened to them and modified his concerns in the light of their demands to be sure. But he was the real enforcer of any submission, overt or intuited. For what, she wondered, did *he* stand—" Samuel R. Delany, *Neveryóna* (New York: Bantam, 1983), pp. 351–352.

6. Delany, *Motion of Light*, p. 5.

7. Delany, *Motion of Light*, p. 15.

8. See, for example, Stanley Crouch, "Play the Right Thing," *New Republic*, 202 no. 7 (Feb. 12, 1990):30–37.

9. Davis, *Miles*, pp. 62,66.

10. Davis, *Miles*, pp. 10, 52.

11. Davis, *Miles*, p. 52.

12. This analysis has benefited from the insights and contributions of Sonya Michel, who was kind enough to continue electronic conversations with me after I presented a paper on Miles Davis at Princeton in 1995.

13. Davis, *Miles*, p. 20.
14. Davis, *Miles*, p. 31. My emphasis.
15. Davis, *Miles*, p. 39.
16. Davis, *Miles*, p. 63.
17. Quincy Troupe has referred to Davis's home life as "moribund." Unpublished paper, presented at Miles Davis Conference, Washington University, St. Louis, MO, April 7, 1995.
18. Davis, *Miles*, p. 256. This conflict between home life and music life is not unique to Davis's situation. See, for example, how a jazz musician gets "crossed up between love for her and the love for your instrument," in Valerie Wilmer, *As Serious As Your Life* (Westport, Conn.: Lawrence Hill, 1980), p. 194.
19. Davis, *Miles*, p. 228.
20. Davis, *Miles*, p. 366.
21. Davis, *Miles*, p. 136.
22. Davis, *Miles*, p. 148.
23. See also how Davis's relationship with Susan Garvin is described in *Miles*, p. 160.
24. Charles Mingus and Nel King, *Beneath the Underdog* (New York: Knopf, 1971), pp. 281–282. Davis hung out with Mingus in Los Angeles in 1946 and became his best friend. See Davis, *Miles*, pp. 91–92.
25. See in particular how Davis describes his mentors' relationships: "Freddie [Webster] had a lot of bitches. Women were his thing, besides music and heroin" (*Miles*, p. 62). See also the scene in the cab with Bird, pp. 65–66.
26. Pearl Cleage, *Deals with the Devil and Other Reasons to Riot* (New York: Ballantine Books, 1993), pp. 41–42. Emphasis original.
27. Quoted in Wilmer, *As Serious As Your Life*, pp. 193, 195.
28. Lorraine Gillespie, quoted in Dizzy Gillespie, *To Be Or Not To Bop* (New York: Doubleday, 1979), pp. 379–380.
29. Gillespie, *To Be or Not to Bop*, p. 189.
30. Sarah Vaughan, quoted in Gillespie, *To Be or Not To Bop*, p. 192.
31. Leo Bersani, *Homos* (Cambridge, MA: Harvard University Press, 1995), p. 6. Emphasis original.
32. Samuel R. Delany, *The Straits of Messina* (Seattle, WA: Serconia Press, 1989), p. 50.
33. Nat Hentoff, *The Jazz Life* (New York: Da Capo Press, 1961), p. 53.
34. For a concise and informative history of these laws and the campaigns to overturn them, see Paul Chevigny, *Gigs: Jazz and the Cabaret Laws in New York City* (New York: Routledge, 1991).
35. Chevigny, *Gigs*, pp. 4, 17, and 58–59.
36. Chevigny, *Gigs*, pp. 60–61.

37. See Davis, *Miles*, pp. 238–240.

38. Davis, *Miles*, p. 240.

39. Delany, *Motion of Light*, p. 267.

40. Delany, *Motion of Light*, p. 268.

41. Delany, *Motion of Light*, pp. 268–269. Emphasis original.

42. Delany, *Motion of Light*, pp. 269–270.

43. Delany, *Motion of Light*, 207.

44. For columns see, for example, Samuel R. Delany, "Atlantis: Model 1924," in *Atlantis: Three Tales* (Hanover, NH: University Press of New England, 1995). For "The Bridge of Lost Desire" see, for example, the Nevèrÿon series.

45. This may explain why Davis's music of the late fifties to sixties has been so important to black women (among whom I include myself), as Pearl Cleage describes in her essay.

46. Davis, *Miles*, p. 183.

47. Mingus, *Beneath the Underdog*, p. 282.

48. Hentoff, *Jazz Life*, p. 27.

49. I am thinking here particularly of his relationship with musicians in the new quintet and sextet.

50. Miles Davis, "Bags' Groove (Take One)," *Bags' Groove*, Prestige (P-7109) OJCCD-245-2. All the recordings I discuss are easily available on CDs. Listening to the music will yield a much richer understanding of my analysis and argument.

51. Eric Nisenson, *'Round About Midnight* (New York: Dial Press, 1982), p. 91.

52. Davis, *Miles*, p. 187.

53. Charles Keil and Steven Feld, *Music Grooves* (Chicago: University of Chicago Press, 1994), pp. 64–65.

54. Keil and Feld, *Music Grooves*, p. 65.

55. The Miles Davis Quintet, "'Round Midnight," *'Round About Midnight*, Columbia CK 40610.

56. J. C. Thomas, *Chasin' the Trane* (New York: Doubleday, 1975), pp. 85, 105–106.

57. Jack Chambers, *Milestones I: The Music and Times of Miles Davis* (New York: William Morrow, 1989), p. 235.

58. Davis, *Miles*, p. 187.

59. Delany, *Motion of Light*, p. 344.

60. Chambers, *Milestones I*, p. 235; Amiri Baraka, *The Music: Reflections on Jazz and Blues* (New York: William Morrow, 1987), p. 300.

61. Herbie Mann, quoted in Hentoff, *Jazz Life*, p. 218.

62. Baraka, *The Music*, p. 293.

63. See Valerie Wilmer's good discussion of "Woman's Role," in chaps. 11 and 12 of *As Serious as Your Life*, from which I have already quoted.

64. Raymond Williams, *The Long Revolution* (New York: Harper and Row, 1961), p. 25.

65. Williams, *Long Revolution*, pp. 24–25. Susan McClary also cites this passage in *Feminine Endings: Music, Gender and Sexuality* (Minneapolis: University of Minnesota Press, 1991), p. 23.

66. Despite feminist insistence that *the personal is political*, it is a characteristic of analyses of jazz that the music is discussed or judged in formalist terms, terms which accept and maintain a conceptual distance between our public and private spheres of existence. It is precisely this distance that Pearl Cleage attempts to close though her act of imaginative empathy and her contemplation of the possibility of an act of public retaliation. This chapter seeks to raise questions about the ways in which we talk about music and musicians and to challenge the assumptions and limitations of formalist analysis from a feminist perspective. I hope to demonstrate the need for a new form of musicology, a music criticism that enables us to understand the formation and dissemination of the gendered meanings produced in jazz, jazz performance, and in critical discourse about jazz.

Methodologies of feminist music criticism offer us a variety of ways to address the limitations of formalist modes of analysis, and I will be drawing freely upon such insights. But I also employ materialist analysis, which seek to track the complex relations that exist between cultural forms and social formations. Music should not be excluded from critical examination using these tools of analysis. Like literature, film, and the visual arts, music both produces and reproduces meaning, and I am particularly interested in how music, in its form and performance, produces and enables gendered and sexual meanings. As Susan McClary has argued: "The codes marking gender difference in music are informed by the prevalent attitudes of their time. But they also themselves participate in social formation, inasmuch as individuals learn how to be gendered beings through their interactions with cultural discourses such as music. Moreover, music does not just passively reflect society; it also serves as a public forum within which various models of gender organization (along with many other aspects of social life) are asserted, adopted, contested and negotiated." In particular, McClary continues, "[m]usic is also very often concerned with the arousing and channeling of desire, with mapping patterns through the medium of sound that resemble those of sexuality." I want to ask how particular aspects of the music of Miles Davis can be seen to map patterns that arouse and channel desire, and to show

how his performance is a public forum "within which various models of gender organization . . . are asserted, adopted, contested and negotiated." See Susan McClary, *Feminine Endings,* pp. 7–8, 25.

67. See Krin Gabbard, "Signifyin(g) the Phallus: *Mo' Better Blues* and Representations of the Jazz Trumpet," *Cinema Journal,* 32, 1 (Fall 1992):43–62. "On the most obvious level," argues Krin Gabbard, "the phallicism of the jazz trumpet resides in pitch, speed, and emotional intensity, all of which Armstrong greatly expanded in the 1920s. The many artists who followed Armstrong have found numerous ways of dealing with this dimension of the trumpet. By contrast the Eurocentric virtuoso who can play high and fast is not necessarily phallic: what a symphony player might call bad technique—an extremely wide vibrato or a 'smeared' note, for example—can become a forceful, even virtuosic device in the hands of a jazz trumpeter. Stage deportment and the musician's clothing can also become part of the phallic style. Consider the pelvic thrusts that Dizzy Gillespie performed in front of his big band in the 1940s, or the 'Prince of Darkness' mode in which Miles Davis clothed himself during his final two decades."

68. In the *Milestones* CD liner notes the recording dates for the album are incorrectly given as February 4 and March 4. They actually are April 2 and 3. Miles Davis, *Milestones,* Columbia, CK 40837.

69. Ian Carr, *Miles Davis: A Biography* (New York: William Morrow, 1982), pp. 93–94.

70. Hentoff, *Jazz Life,* p. 220.

71. Delany, *Motion of Light,* pp. 205–206.

72. Davis, *Miles,* p. 226.

73. Davis, *Miles,* p. 226.

74. J. C. Thomas, *Chasin' the Trane,* p. 109.

75. Bill Evans, "Improvisation in Jazz," liner notes to *Kind of Blue,* p. 2. Columbia CK 40579.

76. Delany, *Motion of Light,* p. 326.

77. Joe Henderson, *So Near, So Far: Musings for Miles,* Verve 314 517 674–2, 1993.

78. Bill Evans, "Improvisation in Jazz," *Kind of Blue.*

79. Joe Goldberg described Davis's group, which was together from the end of 1955 until the spring of 1957, as follows: "At least part of the unique quality of the quintet performances lay in a particular principle which Davis grasped, a principle so simple that it apparently eluded everyone else. To put it in terms of this particular group, a quintet is not always a quintet. It could also be a quartet featuring Miles, and, at different times on the same tune, it could be a quartet featuring Coltrane or a trio featuring either Garland or Chambers. The Davis

rhythm section, Jones in particular, was well aware of this, and gave each of the three principal soloists his own best backing." Joe Goldberg, quoted in Rosenthal, *Hard Bop*, pp. 49–50. I extend this principle to the sextet.

80. I am thinking here, particularly, of the various performances of "My Funny Valentine" and the relationship Davis develops with pianist Herbie Hancock. Much more work remains to be done, but it has begun. See Howard Brofsky, "Miles Davis and *My Funny Valentine*: The Evolution of a Solo," *Black Music Research Journal* (1983):23–45; and the very interesting essay by Robert Walser, "'Out of Notes': Signification, Interpretation and the Problem of Miles Davis," in Krin Gabbard, ed., *Jazz Among the Discourses* (Durham, NC: Duke University Press, 1995), pp. 165–188. Brofsky compares three versions of the tune; Walser concentrates on the 1964 live performance with Herbie Hancock. There are, however, five versions of the tune easily available on CD, three of which are recordings of live performances; comparing them would make a fascinating study. Miles Davis, *Cookin' with the Miles Davis Quintet*, Prestige OJCCD-128-2; *'58 Miles*, Columbia CK 47835; *The Complete Concert 1964*, Columbia C2K 48821; and *Miles Davis the Complete Live at the Plugged Nickel 1965*, Columbia CXK 66955 [a set of seven CDs].

81. Walser, "'Out of Notes,'" p. 167.

82. See, for example, the account of the relationship that Delany and Marilyn Hacker have with Bob in Delany, *Motion of Light*, pp. 380–514, weeks that Delany refers to as the happiest in his life. See also Samuel R. Delany, *Heavenly Breakfast: An Essay on the Winter of Love* (Flint, MI: Bamberger Books, 1997), a reflection on living in urban communes and cooperatives during the winter of 1967–68. Delany's fiction consistently explores the possibilities of challenging familial structures and conventions for sexual unions, but see in particular Samuel R. Delany, *Trouble on Triton* (New York: Bantam Books, 1979), for a story that is based on various forms of cooperative living.

83. Samuel R. Delany, *Silent Interviews: On Language, Race, Sex, Science Fiction and Some Comics* (Hanover, NH: University Press of New England, 1994), p. 26.

6. Lethal Weapons and City Games

1. *Grand Canyon*, Panavision TCF, 1991, dir. Lawrence Kasdan.

2. *Bat 21*, Tri-Star, 1988, dir. Peter Markle.

3. It is clear that this association between the war zones of Southeast Asia and Los Angeles has been established incrementally. Of particular importance to this process are the three *Lethal Weapon* films, which will be discussed later. *Lethal Weapon 3* is a culmination of the themes of the previous two: policing is indistinguishable from military intervention, and the burning of a housing com-

plex is visually evocative of the burning of villages in Vietnam. Our reading of this scene of fire is, of course, directly influenced by *Apocalypse Now*, which reinforces my sense that Hollywood has and continues to mediate and inform this process of transition in the political imagination of the culture industry.

4. Promotional description, *Grand Canyon*, FoxVideo, 1992.

5. Emphasis as spoken.

6. This superficial way of locating Mack is of course a postmodern substitute for history. See Fredric Jameson, *Postmodernism, the Cultural Logic of Late Capitalism* (Durham: Duke University Press, 1991), pp. 6, 67–68.

7. This is a moment in which a scene of home is intercut into the nightmare journey.

8. NWA, *Straight Outta Compton*, Priority Records, 1988, CD 57102. I use the male pronoun here because the lyrics reference a very masculine performativity and sense of prowess.

9. I adopted the term "good guy" because of the following incident. When I was talking to a research assistant at the Video Library in Philadelphia who was helping me locate a copy of one of Danny Glover's early films, *Out*, he reacted with sharp surprise to my description of Glover's role in that film as an urban revolutionary. "But," he said in a shocked tone, "Danny Glover is a good guy!"

10. Perhaps it is crass to point to the biblical resonance of the choice of Simon as a name for Mack's rescuer, but it gains significance through the consistent religious references in the film, particularly its concern with spiritual and miraculous transformation. Kasdan's "gang" take pleasure not only in threatening physical harm but in taunting and mocking Mack. "And they spat upon him, and took the reed, and smote him on the head. And after that they mocked him, they took the robe off from him, and put his own raiment on him, and led him away to crucify him. And as they came out they found a man of Cyrene, Simon by name: him they compelled to bear his cross." Matthew 27, 30–32. Even if the biblical allusion works only at a subliminal level, it is important to recognize that Mack (and the white middle class) are being rescued from a possible crucifixion, a metaphor which has political and ideological meanings. In such a scenario, Mack (and the white middle class) are innocent victims of unjust persecution.

11. *Body and Soul*, Enterprise, 1947, dir. Robert Rossen.

12. *Escape from Alcatraz*, Paramount, 1979, dir. Don Siegel.

13. *Chu Chu and the Philly Flash*, Twentieth Century Fox, 1981, dir. David Lowell Rich.

14. *Out!* (also known as *Deadly Drifter*), an independent production, 1982, dir. Eli Hollander.

15. *Iceman*, Universal, 1984, dir. Fred Schepisi.

16. *Places in the Heart*, Tri-Star, 1984, dir. Robert Benton.

17. *Witness*, Paramount, 1985, dir. Peter Weir.

18. *Silverado*, Lawrence Kasdan, 1985, dir. Lawrence Kasdan.

19. *The Color Purple*, Warner, 1985, dir. Steven Spielberg.

20. Danny Glover's roles as Nelson Mandela in *Mandela*, 1987, and as Micah Mangena in *Bopha!*, 1993, are not discussed, since these films address a very different set of political concerns from those I set out to cover in this book. Glover was also very active in anti-apartheid organizations.

21. *Flight of the Intruder*, Paramount, 1991, dir. John Milius.

22. *Lethal Weapon*, Warner, 1987, dir. Richard Donner; *Lethal Weapon 2*, Warner, 1989, dir. Richard Donner; *Lethal Weapon 3*, Warner, 1992, dir. Richard Donner.

23. See also n. 3.

24. George Harrison, "Cheer Down," Dark Horse Records, lyrics by George Harrison and Tom Petty.

25. I am grateful to Michael Denning for pointing out this literary parallel.

26. Andrew Hacker, *Two Nations: Black, White, Separate, Hostile and Unequal* (New York: Macmillan, 1992), p. 19.

27. Thomas Byrne Edsall, with Mary D. Edsall, *Chain Reaction: The Impact of Race, Rights, and Taxes on American Politics* (New York: Norton, 1992).

28. I have excluded *To Sleep With Anger*, Metro, 1990, dir. Charles Burnett, as being outside of the Hollywood circuit of representations of black men. This fine film, in which Danny Glover not only stars as Harry Mention but also acts as executive director, explores complexities of black subjectivity far beyond Hollywood's limited imagination. His participation in production and his efforts to help finance Spike Lee's *Get on the Bus*, Forty Acres and a Mule, 1996, are evidence of Glover's attempts to move beyond the genealogy that Hollywood has created for him.

ACKNOWLEDGMENTS

Race Men began as "Genealogies of Race, Nation and Manhood," the W. E. B. Du Bois Lectures at Harvard University in 1993. I would like to acknowledge the intellectual generosity of both students and faculty who attended the lectures, receptions, and dinners: their comments and enthusiasm were inspiring. Bill Sisler, who had been my editor for *Reconstructing Womanhood*, persuaded me that these lectures should be reworked as a book for Harvard University Press, and Lindsay Waters has been a very patient editor, providing guidance, support, and encouragement whenever it was needed. His assistant, Kimberly Steere, has efficiently and very warmly responded to my questions, and Anita Safran made good suggestions for stylistic changes.

The staff of the Beinecke Rare Book and Manuscript Library at Yale University ensure that it is truly one of the most wonderful places in the world in which to work. I wish particularly to single out Patricia Willis, Curator of the American Literature Collection, which includes the James Weldon Johnson Collection, for her help, enthusiasm, and friendship. Students and faculty at universities all over the country have generously shared their ideas in response to my presentation of various parts of the book as it was being written, and I am indebted to all of you.

My colleagues in American Studies, in African and African American Studies, and in Women's Studies are a wonderful group of people to whom I owe so much. Nancy Cott and Dolores Hayden remain models of how to be an intellectual *and* a woman at Yale. I am particularly grateful to the members of the American Studies faculty seminar for their readings of an early draft of Chapter 5, on Miles Davis and jazz, and for making invaluable suggestions for its improvement. As always I am deeply indebted to the intellectual generosity, friendship, and support of my students. You are truly an inspiring group of people. Saje Mathieu helped me to find material on Paul Robeson, and Françoise Humphrey tracked down illustrations when I despaired of ever finding them. No one could ever wish for more efficient research assistance—miracles really were accomplished, and I am deeply grateful to you both.

Robert Reid-Pharr introduced me to the work of Essex Hemphill and has, himself, been an important influence on my work. Robert, Paul Gilroy, and Robin Kelley are more than intellectual mentors and friends; their deep commitment to exposing and abolishing patriarchal abuse and exploitation make them a formidable brotherhood. The black feminist vision embodied in the artwork of Deidre Harris Kelley has inspired me for years. I am honored that she agreed to let me use one of her paintings for the cover of this book. Claudia Tate read the first complete draft of Chapter 1, on W. E. B. Du Bois, and I am very grateful for her many helpful suggestions. Jody Lester, Vron Ware, and Susan Willis graciously agreed to read the entire manuscript. Their comments and conversation are and will remain an essential measure for my work.

It is impossible to express the importance of my partnership with Michael Denning and the significance of my intellectual debt to him.

Finally, a word about my black female sisters in the academy among whom are Kathleen Cleaver, Angela Davis, Ann du Cille, Saidiya Hartman, Evelyn Brooks Higginbotham, Lisa Jones, Deborah McDowell, Nellie McKay, Toni Morrison, Nell Irvin Painter, Trisha Rose, and Valerie Smith and with whom I steal precious moments at conferences and professional meetings. Your wisdom, insights, and commitment are with me always.

INDEX